I0408494

CONTENTS

HOW TO CREATE LIKE GOD

God's Success Blueprint For All Creators, Companies & Churches

DEDICATION

I dedicate this book to my family and friends, who have constantly and consistently supported me throughout my creative career. Despite the challenges and uncertainty that comes with any creative project or business, they believed and invested into it nonetheless. Things were tough at the beginning, but this book will change everything forever!

I want to thank you my brother Rodrick for your timely conversational coaching and strategic support, which saw NiyotheGreatest Media Agency (Studios) establish itself as a successful brand and business. Thank you Jack, for all your investments and sacrifices you have made to make me what I am today. The selflessness and sacrifice you have shown is Christ-like beyond words.

Thank you Sam, for believing in me when I did not and watering the seeds of greatness within. Thank you Shadrack, for validating my ideas and thus empowering me, imploring me to live a principled life. Thank you, Joselyne, for being the best sister in the world, for being there for me in my down times and speaking life into my chaos and lifelessness.

Thank you Jean De Dieu for empowering me to face the world. You have always been a source of direction and courage, I appreciate your ever needed business coaching and guidance..

To the rare friends who have always been there, in person and in spirit, constantly pushing me to level up and to never give up. Daniel, Cecille, Amon, Seth, Jeff, Gift, Gershom, Elois, Sarah. I say thank you! You guys are rare.

Finally, thank you, Mama na Papa, for being the best parents in the whole wide world. Thank you for naming me Niyomugabo(God is the Greatest -NiyotheGreatest) I have trully found Him to the the form and substance of life. Without you I would not have been introduced to the Creator of creators, inventor of invention, the source of all wisdom, life and happiness: Imana (God) or, as they say in Zulu -Inkosi ya Makhosi.

Moreover, I also want to dedicate this book to my creator family, those who share the same passion for creating and co-creating with God to expand His kingdom on earth. Your determination to make this a reality is a constant source of inspiration.

SPECIAL THANKS

S pecial thanks to the giants upon whose shoulders I stand. Upon whose brains I build. Thought leaders whose life and work has provided context and content.They have helped me discover my purpose and fully deploy myself. Many people have influenced my thinking and helped me get the courage to embrace my calling, but none have more than these.

Special thanks to Dr. Jordan Peterson for the challenging lectures, eye-opening debates, and appeals. You have challenged me and forced me to be formidable in thought and in word, and train my mind in 'high-resolution thinking'.

Thank you Dr. Myron Goldon, for the insightful and empowering business success Bible studies and wisdom that have seen me fully launch a business and write a book.

Vusi Thembekwayo, your honest and real talk on the principles of success, is revolutionising and galvanising african business leaders. You remain a true inspiration, and when I hear you say, "the old things are true", I get that as a confirmation that indeed the basic principles always beats modern methods that are not grounded in scripture and in God. Hence the writing of this book to expound on the Genesis's blueprint; to ground creators and establish them in the truth. The truth that never changes.

Thank you, Pastor Khethelo Mazibuko, for the profoundly divine messages from God's word that you passionately share. I love listening to your sermons, so dont be surprised if you see some of your concepts shared and developed further in this book.

Thank you Jefferson Bethke for the inspiration to pursue poetry, writing and public speaking. Your poetry and books have really fueled and fired within me a desire to engage more in content creation and share whats on my mind. Thank you for the book 'It's Not What You Think' , 'to Hell with the Hustle' and the masterpiece poem - 'The Greatest Artist of All Time '.

I also want to acknowledge the invisible forces behind my thinking. The incredible works of Myles Munroe -in particular the book , In Pursuit of Purpose, which saw me literally pursue my pupose and lead a purpose driven life. The great works and books of Earl Nightingale like Lead the Field and many more.

In truth, all thoughts are derived from other thoughts, so much so that there is no such thing as original thought.(As the wisest man in Ecclesiastes says - There is Nothing new Under the Sun.) And God ordained it so, that we may not be independent atoms separated from each other but an interconnected, interdependent web of omnipotent prowess.

INTRODUCTION

This book was born out of a quest for clarity. It was born out of years of intense seeking and searching. The goal was to find the secret of success in creativity, productivity, and all creative entreprises or pursuits.

A decade-long experience as a multi-media creator and editor inspired the principles I share in this book. I have worked as a content creator, spoken word artist, video editor, photographer, videographer, drone operator, product manager, music writer and composer and, of course, author and writer. In all these areas of work, one question kept confronting me. How do I know that what I am doing is the right thing to do? How can I ensure that the endeavour and/or project I am working on will succeed?

Is success guesswork and luck, or is it predictable? Are there principles that govern the world of success?

Recently, I launched NiyotheGreatest Media Agency(Studios), a business that helps creators and business owners achieve creative success(success in creativity)—allowing them to create with clarity, confidence and competence. These questions haunted me more. Uncertainty seemed to take complete control in a land that depends on certainty and clarity to function.

How can I guarantee that my business or project will be profitable and impact lives. Especially when everybody else doubts it will, and I am not making enough profits or gains from it. How do I know, I am using the correct business model?

Will I get customers? What if I don't get customers? These ever-present questions led me on a search for all the answers I could find. And so the journey began.

I surfed the internet and binge-watched volumes of youtube videos in search for the blueprint, the pattern, the key to success. From Patrick Bet David to Anthony Oneal to Dave Ramsey to scores of other famous youtubers in the personal development, business, finance and success niches, I listened to all of them.

And although I sensed that these people were sincere and that they knew what they were talking about, the information provided seemed too high level for me to be practical. I needed to have an actionable strategy from listening to their talks.

Sleepless nights and distracted days amounted to more frustration and confusion. But the solution was on the way. One day I saw a video by Myron Golden. His video was different. It was a Bible study. As a Bible enthusiast myself , I knew full well that the Bible is a geat source of success principles and prosperity in general but never was this concept communicated the way Myron did.

Myron Golden is a successful entrepreneur who believes that to build a profitable enterprise, you don't need a good idea; you need a God idea. He emphasizes the importance of having faith and trusting in God's plan for your life rather than relying solely on your own abilities. Golden encourages people to focus on their mindset and to avoid negative thoughts such as worry and anxiety, which can hinder success. He also stresses the importance of learning from successful people and being coachable.

The video from Myron that caught my attention is the one where he shares Solomons's business model and how it made him rich. Everything that was shared made all the sense in the world. And it became my intention to apply these principles and see what would happen to my business as well.

After watching almost half of his youtube content, my heart was content. I felt that this was it. His knowledge was the missing link in my search for the success puzzle. My mindset had already changed at this point, and I started to see things I had never seen before or better put, that I was mental- blocked from seeing before. I reasoned with myself as Myron would and does that if I want to be successful, the answer is to be found in God,

> "For promotion cometh neither from the east, nor from the west, Nor from the south. But God is the judge: He putteth down one, and setteth up another".Psalm 75:6-7

This may seem like an oversimplification of the science of success, but its not. As simple as it may seem and sound, it took me years to finally understand it and fully embrace it. At the end of this book you will agree with me that , this is the most significant success secret of all times.

After wrestling with God and His words for a few intense months , I came about the perfect blueprint for success for all creators. And here is the cool thing, this is not what I heard from Myron, as great as his insight, impact, and experience are.

I heard this from God Himself, the Greatest Artist/ creator of all Times, as Jefferson Bethke would put it. And here is what's more fun, you too have the power and privilege to hear from Him directly. One of the most extraordinary things about imagination or thought is that it does not remain the same when shared. It multiplies.

A thought or an idea is like a seed that is sown in the ground. When you share an idea, you are planting seeds that will potentially yeild 30 fold, 60 fold or 100 fold(I will get to this pattern later in the book)

This is precisely why I am writing this book. This is why this book is worth your time, attention and investment. Ideas are very powerful, way more powerful than you think. More than money, more than matter.

They grow when they are exchanged. This means that when you read what I have written, it won't just be you reading what I have written.What I have written will be multiplied by your experience and expertise, and you will end up with more than what is written here.The only catch is, you must be here first.

It's quite a unique and humbling yet empowering experience and reality. So, take notes, ask intentional high quality questions, as you read, rephrase the ideas and concepts in you own words. This will do more for you more than all the words that my pen can write. It's not about what you know, it's about who you are and what you do with what you know. For ideas to cross the bridge between knowledge and implementation, there has to be this wonderful process of assimilation which involves intentional, internal and intense thinking.

So join me now on this journey to becoming God-Creators, co-creators with God. Creators who create after God's own heart and pattern. Creators who create with a practical purpose, meaningful mission and vivid vision. Creators who create with clarity, confidence and competence in Christ.

In the next few pages, I will be laying down the crucial concepts and profound principles that guide and govern the universe of creative success. I believe that time is more valuable and expensive than money. And I believe this book will save you years' worth of time literally. You will thank me later.

And by the way, If we are just meeting(which is most likely), my name is James Niyomugabo; I am a Creator Coach and founder of NiyotheGreatest Studios.

I was born in **Tanzania**, grew up in **Malawi**, have lived in **South Africa** and currently live in **Canada**, in the beautiful British Columbia province from where I am writing this book.

My mission is to help creators like yourself to create with clarity, confidence and competence, using Christ's comprehensive blueprint and strategy. I do this by providing extensive **creator coaching, collaboration, creator connections, creator courses and speaking engagements**.

Here is a little background about myself.

MY CREATOR JOURNEY

I became aware of my creative gifts when I was about ten years old. At a very young age I knew that I had the gift of speaking, writing and composing.When I went to church and school, the only parts that intersted me where those that involved public speaking or some sorts of brainstorming and composition.

Like other kids I also enjoyed play but my play was different. It was real. My favourite hobby was playing with toys -African toys, to be specific.

In most rural areas in Africa (at least where I come from), children use sticks and stones as toys. I used them to tell stories and replicate scenes I had seen in movies or ones I had originated myself. I did this by assigning each stick a character and then, using my hands, would act out movements and actions using the sticks.

As I moved the sticks around to demonstrate the activity, I would then narate the story describing the scenes. If you saw me you would think I am a professional ventriloquist. My younger siblings and friends would sit down, and then the show would begin. These are the earliest memories of my creativity.

As my vocabulary expanded, my interest in spoken word and public speaking grew as well. I started writing and performing, something that has been kept alive in me ever since.

For context, I was born and raised in a refugee camp. I was born in one, in Tanzania and grew up in another in Malawi. My story , my life has its roots in Dzaleka Refugee Camp, where I spent the first 12 years of my life.

Dzaleka refugee camp is located in Malawi, an hour away from the capital city of Lilongwe. It is the largest refugee camp in Malawi, established by UNHCR in 1994, and is home to more than 50,000 (used to be a lot less back then) refugees and asylum seekers from five different countries. The refugees and asylum seekers in Dzaleka are mainly from the Democratic Republic of the Congo, Burundi, Rwanda, Ethiopia, and Somalia. The camp offers shelter, primary and secondary schools, a health center, and a public market. However, the food rations and resources never seemed to be enough to survive on. And yet the government restricts and punishes any business operations by refugees who leave the camp for other cities in the country.

Creativity is not an option in an environment like this; you have to be creative or starve and die. You have to be creative with how to make a living, preserve food and water, and navigate and work around restrictions and limitations imposed on you. In all honesty, though, my creativity was mostly for fun, since at this age, I didnt have any responsibility but that. I was finding little ways to stay happy in an otherwise not-so-happy place.

Creativity became my escape and saviour. While in Malawi, I became passionate about creating ideas and groups. I co-founded several groups and participated in numerous others. The groups I worked with and that I am most proud are the present Truth Music ministry and Dzaleka Acrobats respectively.

The Present Truth was a music ministry with some of my brothers and friends that sang at churches and other churchrelated events. It was here that I nurtured my love for Acapella music and fell in love with the human voice.

Dzaleka Acrobats is a group of refugee Acrobats in Dzaleka refugee camp that perform gymnastic stunts and styles at various public events in the area. Although I parted with dzaleka Acrobats in 2014.The group still moves on as a living legacy, performing at more significant events and spaces.

Creativity led me to create songs, write some poetry, create groups and start clubs but creativity surprizingly enough also led me to the world of science. I remember early on in school; my favourite subject was natural sciences. When I wasn't creating my little projects, I was busy reading science books and trying out the experiments from the books.

I used to be very interested in these experiments, so much so that once I had a close call with a fire in the science lab. I was testing the reaction between potassium/sodium with water.

I had read that the highly unstable pure sodium or potassium wants to lose an electron, and this splits the water atom, producing a negatively charged hydroxide ion and hydrogen, forming an explosive gas that ignites. So I put potassium into a beaker of water, and it immediately ignited. The scene was lit and cool, filled with excitement but I couldn't extinguish the flames nor the excitement.

Not even with my poetic mouth.

I learnt that day that poets are not that special after all. Despite thier multitude of words they have the same lung capacity as everyone else.

As you can imagine, I became apprehensive. Labs have many flammable substances, and the flames not going off made me anxious that the fire could get out of control. After a few moments of panic, I remembered that blocking the oxygen supply to the reaction would put out the flames. So I covered the beaker with my foot (of all things), and the fire went out.

This story is the story of my life. I have always understood that I have been called to make phenomenal impact through speaking, writing and media-technology. And for most of my life, I have been just experimenting. When I started NiyotheGreatest Studios, it was a cute idea, but I didnt know there would be fire.

I have had business ideas implemented before; when I tried they either failed miserably or simply existed in name only.

But every time there is fire, I go back to the basics and put it off. Going back to zero every time is why I am still here, it is why I am writing this book: the basics: principles,the blueprint. The Bible is filled with these-

Principles of how God operates, works, blesses or even curses— side note when I was in high school at Dzaleka Secondary School.I habitually read books that were above my grade level in the field of biology and physics and geography. As a result, I tended to have some knowledge of subject at hand in class. This , coupled with my love for science experiments, led everyone to call me **Scientist.**

When I moved to South Africa in 2014, my life's focus and direction shifted; I realized I was more into spoken word, public speaking, and content/product creation than I was into science or acrobatics. My scientific disposition was born out of curiosity more than anything. And then perhaps the love for acrobatics was something I did just to stay creative. Acrogymnastics demands creativity and energy for even the simplest of moves.

While in South Africa, life as I knew it faded out, and a new chapter began. I spent most of my three years there, writing. Most of my proudest spoken word pieces were born in this place. My First poetry anthology - **God Does Not Believe in Atheists-** featured these poems. By the way, if you haven't read or heard them, I invite you to check them out. This anthology will change your life for the rest of your life.

When I moved to Canada in 2017, for the first time I had access to 24-7 Internet and WIFI , and as a consequence access to more creative tools and connection with like-minded creators. It was the most pivotal part of finding and distinguishing myself in my creative career.

Although Canada provided these fantastic opportunities for

personal growth and development, it was not without its challenges and resistance. It is here that reality paused its most challenging questions.The same old questions that all creators face. How do I know I am on the right track? How do I create with clarity and confidence, and competence? How can I become more competent and in control? How do I create products and services that make a difference?

In an age where everybody has a social media account fighting for fame and a name, endless products and services that are highly competitive. How do I distinguish myself, my voice and my brand? How do I make myself relevant in this fluid and oversaturated market?

It took me another five years to truly and fully find myself and my purpose. Finally, I figured it out!

Over the years, I have created several brands and run different youtube channels and other social media accounts. I knew I had a message to share but then I had to find the best medium to do so. This is what led me to media. So I went all in on youtube and video editing and audio engineering and graphic design.

For the past five years, I have worked with several clients, brands, ministries and churches in the creator space, helping them bring their work to the next level. In this book, I break down **the secret to finding your purpose as a creator through God's Creative process** and success blueprint—that is what this book answers in practical principles and steps.

WHO THIS BOOK IS FOR

This book is for all creators who want to create an eternal difference and impact in this world and in the world to come. This is a gift to the creators who have tried all the methods and strategies the world has to offer and still have not been able to pinpoint their purpose. For those who want to level up their creative game in business, relationships and personal development.

On some deep level, this book is for all of us, because we were all created in the image of the creator of all creators - God.

Genesis 1:26 "And God said, let us make man in our **image** after our own **likeness**, and let them have dominion..."

The Image of God means His reflection, His character (moral attributes)and the likeness of God means His mannerisms or functional attributes. One of the main aspects of God's functional attributes is that He is a creator. He is creative. In making us in His image, He made us with this characteristic. This is why for us to experience maximum success, we must do things like Him. (the same ways He does things). This book is part of the Imago Dei Everyday series that features books that will teach you practical principles on how to do things God's way. The titles in this series include- 'How to Create Like God', 'How to Love Like God', 'How To Think Like God', 'How to Eat Like God', 'How To Dress Like God',

'How To Heal Like God', 'How to Sell Like God' and a bonus book called 'God Is- How God is reflected in everyday life'.

Back to our concept.

We were created to create. And the cool thing about this is that When you create like God, you are also destined to succeed like Him. God never fails, His word cannot fail, and God's ways will not fail. Therefore when you create using God's creative blueprint, success is guaranteed- it always works.

I hope you're ready to take your Creative journey to the next level. Whether you're a musician, whether you're you are a podcaster, whether you're YouTuber, whether you are a singer, whether you're a writer, or you have a business with a product that is designed to change the world. Whatever it is that you create, this book is designed specifically for you. So, fasten your seatbelt as we take off and time travel back to when all things began, to find out the best way to begin ours.

CHAPTER 1: IN THE BEGINNING, GOD

"In the beginning God created the heaven and the earth." Genesis 1:1

Before we talk about the crux of God's creative strategy and design, there are a few prerequisites we have to cover. To be part of and excel in God's creative system, you can't just use it anyhow and expect to get something out of it. You must have the right mindset and be in the right context for competent creation to take place. Getting these right is none-negotiable.

The first two chapters of this book will be dedicated to establishing and expounding on these prerequisites. We will discuss them in some depth and detail, as much as pen and paper will allow, and then we should be ready to jump onto the canvas and create awesomeness.

Genesis is indeed a fundamental and foundational book. It is upon this book that the entire canon of the Bible rests and is grounded. Genesis is so deep and thorough that not only is it the bedrock of the Bible but really of the whole world. It gives context to the cosmos. Everything begins in Genesis. It's the go-to book for understanding where we came from, why we are here and where we are going.

Given all the most critical power and function this book has, Genesis is the first and primary book every human should read and understand to be fitted for success in this life and the life to come. The principles I will share in this book are mostly based on the book of Genesis. Remember the premise. If God is the greatest creator of all times, then if we want to create bigger, brighter and better, then we must follow His blueprint.

This book provides exactly that. This book is a snapshot of God's creative strategy and blueprint, to give all creators the mindset and toolsets they need to create assets according to God's design and purpose.

The verse "In the beginning God created heaven and the earth." tells us the story of how God, in the beginning, created everything. For the first time ever, we are introduced to the concept and context of God. Not much is said about Him, making the few that is , exponentially profound. We know from the rest of scriptures that God is self-sufficient, self-existent and dependent on no one for His existence. The name Jehovah means precisely that.

God is the only being that exists out of time, space and matter. We will get to that matter shortly. God created and yet was not created. He is the beginning in whom the beginning began. To put it poetically, in the beginning of beginning, the beginner of beginning began the beginning before the beginning began.

That's how beautiful the story of our Genesis and our creation is. Our life and existence is not the result of randomized evolutionary probabilities. Our beginning comes from precise potential and Divine certainty. We are here because of intentional, intelligent design.

The primary principle we see in Genesis 1:1 is the principle I would like to call **In the beginning, God**. To put it in better terminology, let's call it the principle of the primacy and priority of God. In the beginning God, is a principle that states that everything begins in God. From this axiom it follows that whatever it is that you begin/create as a creature-creator must begin and be founded in God. In other words, before you begin, you must consult God first, since your existence, life, purpose, dreams, and death are in God.

The principle "in the beginning God…" means putting God first in all that you do. This principle is so essential that it is encoded in the Ten Commandments, coming up at number 1.

God says, **"Thou shall not have any other gods before me,"** meaning, He is to be first, best and last in everything. When you think about it, that's the right relationship we ought to maintain with God for us actually to be successful and optimal. We can't experience meaning in this life apart from this.

I am sure you are asking yourself, why is this the case? Why can't I or someone and or something else be first? This is where we need to understand the major distinction between God and the rest of us. We are created beings; God on the other hand is the Creator. By default, it gives Him the right and responsibility to ensure our harmonious sustenance and maintenance. Revelation 4:11 says that He is worthy of our worship and praise because He created all things:

> *"Thou art worthy, O Lord, to receive glory and honour and power: for thou hast created all things, and for thy pleasure, they are and were created."*

Think of the relationship between a parent and a child for a moment. As a parent bringing a child into the world, it is his/her responsibility to guide and lead the child, educate and teach the child until they are grown and able to take care of themselves. It is equally the responsibility of the child to listen and learn from the parent since they know nothing of this world.

Here is the powerful part, if for any moment, that dynamic relationship is lost, that is, if the parent ignores his responsibility or the child does not view their parent as an authority and experience, then trouble ensues. This is actually why the world is in chaos and confusion today. We have so many fathers/parents who have lost touch with their children and vice versa.

Since the children need parenthood, guidance and guardianship by design, when they cannot find it they look for it elsewhere; this ultimately leads them to take lead and replace their parents. Such is the case with God. If we lose touch with Him, we are doomed to overthrow and usurp Him and end up becoming our own gods.

God says, thou shalt not have any other gods before me!

We have to recognize God as the creator and relate to Him as such. He is the source of life, health, wealth and peace. He is the inventor of what we know as reality. This principle is so significant that when Jesus Christ appears on the scene, He says, '

Seek ye first the kingdom of God and His righteousness, and all these things shall be added to you.' Matthew 6:33

There is power in seeking God first, because when you seek Him first, everything else follows. Everything originates and is derived from Him. **Therefore in a cute sense seeking God is seeking everything.** He is the only person worth seeking because everything else originates from Him.

If you seek your success, if you seek promotion, if you seek the generation of wealth, **and you seek that first** before God, what happens is that, it becomes your god. Then you start worshiping your business, your creativity, and your ideas. This is the reason why you have to seek God **first.** When you don't seek God **first,** you are in danger of seeking yourself **first.** And when you don't relate to God as a creator, being a creature, you cannot maintain sanity, which I'll touch upon more in chapter 2.

For a creature to maintain its being, structure, shape, and form, the creature must relate to the creator in the right relations. In other words, for a creature to exist, it must be connected to its creator. If you separate the creature from the creator, the creature dies. This is very evident in how we create things today. For example, let's consider the almost ubiquitous smartphone. Smart phones are the inventions of humans, created by humans. The smartphone is run by hardware and software. If the creators smartphone do not have a way to maintain and manage the software, eventually, the software dies out; the smartphone becomes unusable, stagnant and un-updatable. Everything that's created must be connected to whoever created it for that created thing to maintain its function, purpose, vision, and mission. After all, it is the creator/manufacturer who defines the purpose of the creature/product.

One of the missing attributes in creatures, in particular humans, is the privilege of infinity. I call it a privilege because it belongs only to God. We are finite beings,and being finite, for us to remain safe, sane, and strong, we have to maintain a connection with our creator; God. When we don't have this connection, we crumble and die.

Being finite and created to need and want God, without Him, we tend to replace Him. We replace God with things, with ideas, with creativity, but ultimately, we replace God with ourselves. Case in point Lucifer.

Ezekiel 28 and Isaiah 14 tell us about this majestic being created by God, named Lucifer. Lucifer means the light bearer. He carried so much light and knowlegde about God that He was at the top of the angelic host and had the privilege of being the most closest of creatures to God. But even though he was privileged with all these things, he did not maintain the right relationship and relation to God. He wanted to be God. The Bible says he was "corrupted by reason of his beauty". Instead of looking to God as the ultimate expression of beauty and good,

Lucifer looked to himself as the ultimate expression of beauty and good; sin was born as a result.

Lucifer sought himself and his own gain instead of seeking God first.

The obvious lesson we lean from this example is that, as business owners and creatives, our job is not to seek success, prosperity or to seek change and make an impact in this world. Our job is much more to seek God, because all these things we are looking for are found in God and only found in the right form and format in Him.

If we choose to get these things aside from God, we will end up creating more misery and pain than is necessary, because the way God has created this world is that there's a principle: **in the beginning, there has to be God**. In the beginning, God has to begin for anything to have a proper end. It must be initiated by and in God, because He is the Alpha and the Omega, the beginning and the end. Therefore before your business, family, and relationships, make sure that it's God first.

Another compelling incentive why we should seek and put God first is that it's only He who guarantees our success. A profound case study that showcases this most strikingly is one that we find in John 21.

In John 21, the disciples had been fishing all night and had caught nothing, Jesus appears on the shore and tells them to cast their net on the right side of the boat. The disciples follow Jesus' instructions and are unable to haul-in the net because of the great number of fish they catch. The story is found in both Luke 5:4-6 and John 21:6-8.

This narrative of experienced fishermen is not only an enlightening post-resurrection account but serves as a deep lesson for all who venture into the vast ocean of creation and aspiration. As the story unfolds, we see these fishermen engrossed in a familiar endeavour, hoping for a bountiful catch after a long night of casting their nets. The darkness envelops them, both literally and metaphorically, as they grapple with the disappointment of empty nets. Their efforts, despite their expertise, bear no fruit, and the sea remains unyielding.

The story takes a transformative turn with the break of dawn. As morning light washes over them, a figure emerges on the shore — Jesus, though they do not recognize Him at first. He offers a simple yet profound directive:

> *"Cast the net on the right side of the ship, and ye shall find."*

Now, it's essential to consider the state of mind of these fishermen. They've exhausted their skills, tried all their known tactics, and might have even explored both sides of the boat. The left side and the right side all would have been familiar territories to them. But the significance of this narrative is not about which side of the boat they've already tried. It's about the transformative power of **divine directive.**

Following the instruction, the fishermen cast their nets and are met with an astonishing reward. Their nets, once barren through the night, are now teeming with fish to the point of breaking. You can imagine the surprise on their faces and the joy in their hearts. This miraculous catch symbolizes more than just material abundance. It represents the unparalleled rewards of aligning one's actions with divine direction.

The story imparts several layers of wisdom. First, it underscores the idea that human effort, devoid of divine guidance, leads to fruitless results. The fishermen were not novices; they were seasoned experts in their trade. Yet, their expertise couldn't guarantee success. Similarly, in our endeavours, be they entrepreneurial, artistic, or personal, we might cast our nets into waters that seem promising, utilizing all our skills and knowledge, only to come up empty. Such moments of barrenness, while disheartening, are also moments of profound introspection. We have to ask ourselves are we relying on human power or divine authority.

Secondly, the narrative teaches that divine direction often comes when we least expect it and in ways we might not immediately recognize. The fishermen did not recognize Jesus initially. Similarly, divine guidance in our lives might come from unexpected sources or at unexpected times. The challenge lies in being receptive, tuning our senses to recognize it, and more importantly, acting upon it.

Lastly, and perhaps most significantly, the story highlights that success is not always about changing the entire strategy or seeking entirely new waters. Sometimes, it's about making subtle shifts, influenced by divine wisdom. Casting the net on the "**right side**" symbolized alignment with a higher will, rather than a drastic change in tactic.

In essence, the story of the fishermen is a timeless parable on the nature of success. It serves as a gentle reminder that in our vast expanse of possibilities and endeavors, finding the right path often requires pausing, listening, and aligning ourselves with a guidance greater than our own wisdom. It's in this harmonious alignment that true success, both material and spiritual, is found.

How are you going to put God first in your projects/products/ services ?

CHAPTER 2:TIME AND SPACE MATTERS

"In the beginning God created the heaven and the earth."Gen 1:1

In the grand theatre of existence, we, as creators, occupy a unique role. Whether we are content creators, video editors, musicians, business owners, entrepreneurs, or any other form of creative expression, we are all expressions of a profound truth: We are creatures; we were created. But this reality, while simple, is fraught with implications that can leave us wrestling with a deep existential unease.

Many of us may wonder why we are here and what our purpose might be. This is not an arbitrary existential inquiry but an exploration born out of our inherent condition as creatures. We did not always exist. There was a moment in time when we 'came into being,' but this does not automatically give us the right or a sense of deserving to be here. It merely underlines our creaturehood, emphasizing our essential dependency, limitations, and our yearning for purpose and meaning.

The first step in grappling with this complexity is a keen awareness of our origins. We must comprehend the blueprint of our existence and recognize the divine reference points from which we emerge. A creature is not a self-sustaining entity. It needs to understand its roots, its 'who,' 'what,' and 'where.' It needs to comprehend its nature and purpose within the greater divine order. God does not need to discover Himself, but we do. As creatures, we develop and change while God remains immutable.

The very nature of our creaturehood makes us vulnerable, confined by limitations on various levels. We can only do, say, and think to the extent of our capacity, and this capacity is restricted by various physical, mental, and temporal constraints. For instance, the dream of humans flying with wings remains just that - a dream - unless we harness the power of technology. We can't simply spread our arms and take off into the heavens because we're limited by our physiological makeup. Such limitations characterize our existence and shape our experience of reality.

Understanding this, let's turn to Genesis 1:1, a verse that profoundly illustrates God's strategy for creating and maintaining sanity in existence. It reads: "**In the beginning, God created the heavens and the earth.**" This sentence is a blueprint of the divine creation process and reflects God's strategies for ensuring sanity in all aspects of life, whether personal, relational, or professional. To maintain sanity, you need structure. Insanity occurs when there is a mismatch between your internal structure and external reality.

In this divine blueprint, God employs three crucial elements to create and sustain existence: **Time**, **Space**, and **Matter**. Let's delve deeper into each of these to understand their importance in our lives and the creative processes.

Time: The Boundary of Duration

Time is the first element that God created, and it remains the first step towards sanity. Time is the boundary of duration, providing a structure that keeps us grounded, stopping us from spiralling into the confusion of eternity. When you go back in time there's no endpoint, similary when you go forward into the future there is no end. It's an infinite regression that our finite minds cannot comprehend. This inconceivable nature of eternity presents a problem for us as creatures - without time, we'd be perpetually disoriented.

Recognizing this, time becomes a valuable resource. Time, in this context, is the currency through which our existence finds meaning. It frames our life, shaping our routines, setting our rhythms, and establishing the stages of our development. We measure our lives in years, months, days, hours, minutes, and seconds, and this measurement grants us a sense of control and comprehension.

Take your creative process, for instance. You need time to conceive an idea, time to bring it into being, and time to refine and perfect it. Time gives you the framework to plan and execute your tasks, allowing you to manage your resources effectively.

God Himself exemplified this. After creating for six days, He rested on the seventh. Each day, He paused and reflected on His work, declaring it good. This rhythm of work and rest is essential for maintaining sanity, and it's a rhythm we ought to emulate.

It's crucial to remember that time isn't your enemy. Time isn't running against you; it's running for you and with you. You just need to learn to learn how to embrace it, to be time conscious. This consciousness provides you with alignment, clarity, focus and purpose.

Space: The Boundary of Places

After creating time, God set about forming the heavens and the earth - space. This spatial boundary ensures we aren't overwhelmed by the incomprehensible vastness of the universe. Just as we grapple with the concept of eternity, we also struggle with the idea of spatial infinity. Does the universe have an end? And if it does, what lies beyond that end?

To prevent us from being overwhelmed by these questions, God created 'space' – the environment, the atmosphere, the sphere in which we exist. In Genesis, we're told that God separated the waters above from those below, grouped the waters into seas, and caused dry land to appear. He established domains within which existence would be not just possible, but efficient.

Similarly, as a creator, you need to define your space. What's your sphere of influence? What's your niche? Defining these gives your creative pursuits structure and direction. Just as space gives physical boundaries to existence, defining your creative space provides boundaries to your imagination and output.

Whether you're a video editor, a musician, a business owner, or an entrepreneur, you have to set boundaries for your work. These boundaries can be in terms of what type of content you create, what industries you cater to, what themes and styles you adhere to, and so on. They give you a unique identity and ensure that your creative output is distinctive and focused.

Matter: The Boundary of Things(Form)

Finally, God created matter. Matter is tangible; it's something we can touch, feel, and interact with. It represents a new level of existence, something that didn't necessarily exist before, not that the other two elements existed before. Matter is essential because it provides boundaries to our physical existence.

If time gives us the boundary of duration and space the boundary of environment, matter provides the boundary of form. It defines the physical parameters within which we operate. Our bodies are matter, giving us a tangible presence in the world. The world around us is also made of matter, creating an environment we can interact with.

In the creative process, matter is what you produce. It's the product of your time and your space. It's the blog post you write, the song you compose, the video you edit, or the business you build. It's the thing that has form and substance, which others can interact with, engage with, and benefit from.

God formed the earth and then populated it with a variety of living creatures, each a unique form of matter. He didn't just create an empty world; He filled it with substance. The same is expected of us. As creators, we're not just tasked with occupying time and space. We're meant to fill them with matter – our work, our creativity, our innovation.Fill the time and space with things that matter.

But to create matter effectively, we need to understand its essential nature. Matter isn't static. It evolves, changes, grows, and adapts. In fact it is by no chance that matter is made up of three states , Solid, Liquid and Gas. When God created the earth, He didn't just make a lifeless rock. He created an environment that could support and sustain life, one that would continue to grow and evolve.

This is a critical lesson for creators. Your creations aren't meant to be static. They're meant to evolve, to grow, to adapt to changing circumstances. This is the true nature of creativity. You're not just producing a thing; you're giving birth to something that has a life of its own.

Applying The Time, Space and Matter Principles To Your Creative Process

Having understood the importance of time, space, and matter in God's creative process, let's look at how you can apply these concepts in your own creativity.

1. Redeem The Time:

God took six days to create the world, taking the time to ensure everything was 'good' before moving on. Take the same approach with your creative process. Don't rush. Take the time you need to ensure your work is the best it can be. Use time as a resource, allowing it to guide your process rather than pressure it.

Create a routine that balances work and rest, just as God did. Understand that rest isn't a waste of time but a critical part of the creative process. It's during rest that your subconscious works on the problems your conscious mind can't solve. Rest is when inspiration often strikes, so embrace it as an essential part of your creative rhythm.

Create schedules and routines to make the most of your time and hold yourself accountable to how you use your time.For every task or activity you do.Ask yourself, how can I do this faster and better? It may mean you need to hire someone else to do it, it may mean you have to use a particular tool or software to save time.Whatever you can do to save you time, do it.

How are you going to redeem your time?

2. Define Your Space:

God separated the heavens from the earth, defining the spaces in which life would exist. In your creative work, identify your niche and stick to it. Know your audience, understand what they need and want, and focus your creativity on meeting those needs and wants.

Create a physical space that inspires creativity.

Your environment greatly influences your mindset and mood, so make sure it's conducive to your work. Whether it's a home office, a studio, or a café, choose a space that helps you focus and generate ideas.

What audience have you been called to serve?

What is the most conducive environment for you to work in?

3. Create Matter That Matters:

When God created the world, He filled it with living creatures, each with a purpose and a role to play. In the same way, ensure your creations have a purpose and add value to the world. Don't create for the sake of creating, but to meet a need, to solve a problem, and to bring joy to others.

Remember that your creations will take on a life of their own. They'll evolve and grow as they interact with the world, just as living creatures do. Embrace this evolution, and be open to feedback and change. Your work is not static; it's dynamic, just like God's creation.

What product/project/service do you have to offer to your audience?

In conclusion, understanding these three main elements of creation empowers you as a creator. It teaches you the value of time, the importance of defining your space, and the purpose of creating matter that matters. Just as God used these elements to create and sustain the universe, you can use them to create and sustain your creative work. Embrace your role as a creator, and strive to create as God does.

CHAPTER 3: WITHOUT FORM AND VOID

"And the earth was without form and void, and darkness was upon the face of the deep." Genesis 1:2

You may be familiar with the phrase 'Without Form and Void' already. It sounds ancient and mystical but how does it factor into God's blueprint for success in creation? Why is it relevant to you as a creator?

The premise of this book, is that every word, every phrase, and every concept introduced in the Bible is not arbitrary. It is mentioned purposefully, with intention, for our learning and guidance. Every single verse is a masterclass for creators and holds timeless wisdom on how to create like the greatest creator of all times, God himself.

Let's start by revisiting the first verse of Genesis: "**In the beginning, God created the Heaven and the Earth.**" This verse, while seemingly straightforward, encapsulates the entire story of creation. It represents the grand blueprint God had in mind before He embarked on the process of creation.

The lesson for creators here is that God didn't create

haphazardly or aimlessly. He had crystal-clear clarity and vision for what He wanted to create. He knew His end goal - Heaven and Earth - before He started. This vision guided His actions. The principle is crucial in any creative process: have clarity of vision.

What is it that you want to create? Do you have a precise picture of it in your mind? Have you written it down? Are you clear about the niche and domain that your idea, product, or solution fits into?

Let's dive deeper into the concept of "without form and void." "Without form and void" is a state of emptiness, a vast expanse of nothingness. It's the blank canvas before a painter, the empty stage before a performer, the blank document before a writer, and the raw material before a craftsman. It's the state of endless possibilities, of potential energy before it is converted into kinetic energy. Every creator encounters this phase: an initial state of nothingness.

This is where we often encounter our first stumbling block. Many of us find this stage intimidating. After all, it's human nature to fear the unknown. But what if we started viewing this state not as an obstacle, but as an opportunity? A blank canvas, an empty page, a raw piece of material - these are all opportunities to create, to bring something new and meaningful into the world. That's the beauty and power of creation: turning one thing into another and viceversa.

When we do this we echo God's first act of creation. From a state of formless void, He created the universe, filling the void with life and purpose. This teaches us that no matter how daunting or complex a task may seem, nothing is too insignificant or grand to be created. There's no void too deep or wide that can't be filled. Every problem or challenge presents an opportunity for creation.

As creators, how do we approach this state of "without form and void?" The answer lies in understanding and accepting it.

It's crucial to recognize and acknowledge the void we're trying to fill or the problem we're trying to solve before we can take steps towards creating a solution. This concept is particularly relevant for entrepreneurs and business owners.

To create effective solutions, you must first understand the gap in the market, the missing link in society, and then create to fill that gap.

This understanding calls for a level of empathy and insight. We must fully comprehend the problem, 'feel' the void we aim to fill, understand the 'darkness' we wish to illuminate and recognize the formlessness that needs to be given form. Only then can we devise an effective solution.

Let's put this concept into perspective with a contemporary example. Consider our modern world, saturated with digital products and services. Every day, new applications are developed, each fulfilling a specific need or solving a specific problem. We live in an era dominated by subscription services, from essential utilities like phone bills and internet services to artificial intelligence apps like ChatGPT Plus, entertainment platforms like Netflix, Amazon Prime and productivity tools like Google Workspace, Zoom and many more .

While these services undoubtedly make our lives easier, they also pose a problem: subscription overload. With each new service we subscribe to, we add another monthly or yearly payment to our budget. Over time, these small amounts can add up to a significant financial burden. Worse yet, it's easy to lose track of all these subscriptions, some of which may be rarely used or even forgotten.

The problem here is clear: the need for an efficient way to manage multiple subscriptions to avoid unnecessary spending. Recognizing this void paves the way for a solution: a subscription management system. This tool would allow users to track all their subscriptions in one place, reminding them of upcoming payments and even suggesting cancellations for rarely used services, It's important to note that the shape and form of the solution (the subscription management system in this case) is directly determined by the nature of the problem (the subscription overload). The void dictates what form the solution should take. The formlessness guides us to the form that needs to be created.

Before we move on to the next chapter, take a moment to write down the problem you are trying to solve, the void you are trying to fill. The more specific and detailed you can be, the better. Remember, recognizing and understanding the void is the first step in the creative process. It's the launching pad from which we can take off and start creating meaningful, impactful solutions, much like God did when He created the world out of a state "without form and void."

What problem are you here to solve?

CHAPTER 4: WHEN THE SPIRIT MOVES

"And the Spirit of God moved upon the face of the waters."
Genesis 1:2

The second thing we hear after God specifies the problem is yet another dreaded but perhaps the most profound stage of the creative process. It says that "the spirit of God moved upon the face of the waters."

From the previous chapter and principle, we explored the significance of understanding the void and knowing the problem you want to solve. Still, the following stage takes it to the next level. The spirit now ventures into the void, he contends with the darkness, and without fear, launches into the deep. As He contends with the darkness and void , something extraordinary happens ; we will dissect that in chapter 5 but for now lets consider the lesson for us to learn in this initial instance. After recognizing the void, the following principle for creators is to explore the void, meet it, feel the darkness, and explore the depth, height and width of what they are dealing with. You could say that this second principle and stage of God's creative process is the somewhat similar to the principle of specifying and understanding the void, but there is a critical contrast I would like to highlight. In the first principle, we see and understand the void based on our knowledge and experience. But more than experience or expertise is needed to solve a problem successfully.

In the second stage we contend with the void and dive into it. We explore the darkness and feel it. We understand the problem from the problem's perspective or the perspective of those going through the problem.

Here we spend time daily contending with the problem we want to solve.When we do this, the answer or solution is inevitable. The rule is that if you contend with a problem long enough, you will eventually get the solution. This is expressed more clearly in the New Testament, where Jesus says,

> "Ask, and it shall be given you; seek, and ye shall find; knock, and it shall be opened unto you:" Matthew 7:7

So when you as a creator contends with a problem long enough and strong enough, you are destined for inspiration. You come into contact with the same spirit that moved upon the face of the waters into the deep darkness. As I write this, a cool quote flashes in my mind that I would like to drop here for you for further thought. It's from a book called Education by Ellen G White; I highly recommend the read; on page 15, it says,

> "Whatever line of investigation we pursue, with a sincere purpose to arrive at truth, we are brought in touch with the unseen, mighty Intelligence that is working in and through all. The mind of man is brought into communion with the mind of God, the finite with the Infinite. The effect of such communion on body and mind and soul is beyond estimate." Education page 15

Thats what I call inspiration. Inspiratus, as the root Latin word would have it, 'breathe into.' But the key to this inspiration is 1. the contending, the research and investigation and 2. sincerity and pursuit of truth.

Most people see and think of inspiration as something that happens accidentally and or is only accessible to genius minds with higher IQ levels. They think inspiration occasionally happens whenever it wants to. Quite oppositely, inspiration is not accidental. You can position yourself to maximize your contact with inspiration.

You must expose yourself to the formlessness and void you want to solve. And if you expose yourself to the formlessness and the void long enough, you will, in no time, come in contact with the amazing power of inspiration, the Holy Spirit Himself. When you expose yourself to the void, you will start recognizing patterns and paths to the solution.

Your brain is optimized for problem-solving and finding solutions; scientific research supports this remarkable capability. Numerous studies have demonstrated the brain's inherent capacity to analyze complex situations, identify patterns, and generate creative solutions. For instance, the brain engages in a remarkable process called pattern completion.

Pattern completion is a cognitive process where the brain fills in missing information based on previously encountered patterns. It helps us recognize and complete familiar patterns or sequences, allowing us to make sense of incomplete or ambiguous stimuli. This process relies on memory retrieval and the activation of stored knowledge. The hippocampus, a brain region involved in memory, plays a significant role in pattern completion. Overall, pattern completion enables us to understand the world, make predictions, and form coherent representations by filling in gaps in our perception.

In addition to pattern completion, the brain utilizes various cognitive processes in problem-solving and innovation. One important process is divergent thinking, which involves generating multiple ideas, possibilities, and solutions. It allows the brain to explore different perspectives and break away from conventional thinking. Another crucial process is cognitive flexibility, which refers to adapting and shifting thinking between different concepts or strategies. It enables the brain to approach problems from different angles and consider alternative approaches.

These cognitive processes work together to facilitate problem-solving and foster creative thinking and innovation.

By the way, this is the reason why we have dreams. Dreams are the ultimate form of inspiration. When you dream your mind gets flooded with tons of information and imagination at once.

There are varied explanations for dreams, from scientific to spiritual. I would like us to focus more on the psychological.

Dreaming is an attempt to venture and navigate the unknown. I heard this idea from psychologist Jordan Peterson, and it made all the sense to me. That's why you have dreams -to help resolve and explain daily discrepancies and navigate unknown territories and threats.

Jordan Peterson, a clinical psychologist, has discussed the connection between dreams and creativity in various talks. According to Peterson, dreams are a way for the unconscious mind to communicate with the conscious mind. They can reveal things about ourselves that we may not be aware of, such as our fears, desires, and unresolved issues. Dreams can also be a source of inspiration for creative endeavors. Peterson suggests that the images and symbols that appear in dreams can be used as a starting point for artistic expression.

Peterson notes that dreams can help us to process and integrate our experiences. Dreams often involve themes and motifs that are related to our waking life, and by exploring these connections, we can gain insight into our own psychology. Peterson also suggests that creativity is closely linked to openness to experience, which is one of the Big Five personality traits. Creative people are more likely to be open to new experiences and to explore the unknown, which can lead to novel insights and ideas.

Overall, Peterson's view is that dreams can be a valuable source of information and inspiration for creative individuals who are willing to explore their own unconscious mind.

In his Why We Sleep book, sleep-expert Mathew Walker suggests that our brains are most active and creative when we are in the dream state. Speaking of sleep and books, my sister, a Sleep Science Coach and Registered Nurse, published her book on the necessity of sleep - entitled Sleep Tight.

"Sleep Tight: The Number 1 Secret to Achieving your Dreams" by Joselyne John is a groundbreaking book that holds immense value for creatives and creators. By seamlessly integrating proven holistic sleep strategies, soothing meditations, and engaging journaling prompts, this book offers a unique approach to enhancing sleep and unlocking the creative potential within. It provides practical advice and techniques specifically tailored to support the creative process, making it a must-read for artists, writers, and anyone seeking to tap into their creative abilities.

With its emphasis on creating a peaceful bedtime routine and harnessing the power of dreams, "Sleep Tight" offers creatives a powerful tool to promote wonder, inspiration, and relaxation, ultimately helping them achieve their artistic goals. This book is a game-changer for creatives, providing them with the tools and insights needed to optimize their sleep and unlock their creative potential.

I recommend this book to all creators.

Now back to inspiration.

The intentionality and design behind dreaming show and prove that inspiration is not accidental. In fact, Inspiration has a purpose, and the purpose of inspiration is to solve a problem. The purpose of inspiration is to optimize, improve, to maximize. That's the purpose of inspiration. So, if you want to have inspiration, expose yourself to the void. Expose yourself to formlessness, and expose yourself to the problems that you want to solve.

Every groundbreaking invention we enjoy today, from the light bulb to the car, from the airplane to the remarkable ChatGPT, emerged from a wellspring of inspiration. These outstanding achievements resulted from individuals deeply attuned to the challenges of their time, immersing themselves in the problems at hand. Through this immersive process, inspiration struck, paving the way for revolutionary solutions and pushing the boundaries of human ingenuity.

Inspiration is an answer to prayer. Inspiration answers the need, want or void we wish to solve. So spend time with a void. Do not be afraid of the darkness.

However much there is darkness upon the face of the deep, launch into it. Do not be scared of the dark world. Feel free to know what it takes. Solve the problem that needs to solved.

What problem were you sent to solve? What difference do you want to make? You may be intimidated by it. Learn to face it because you will only get inspiration when you launch into it without fear.

So, I trust that in this next stage of God's creative process, you have voiced the void, that you have ventured into the void, and now are ready to speak to the void.

Inspiration is not something that we create. Inspiration, as I said, is an answer to prayer. God has inspired you with the solution, but if you're not in the right proximity to the problem to be solved, you will miss the opportunity to make a difference in the lives of those you have been called to serve. You have to come to the problem close enough for you to see the inspiration, for you to see the solution.

What problem are you passionate about?

CHAPTER 5:
THOUGHTS INTO
WORDS

"And God said, Let there be light: and there was light." Genesis 1:3

We just saw how the Spirit of God moved upon the face of the waters, and darkness was upon the face of the deep. The spirit of God wasn't afraid to launch into the darkness and formlessness. He got a feel of the void before any inspiration could happen. And then inspiration did happen. When you have that inspiration from God, the next stage of the creative process is to put the inspiration into words.

Before I break down how that works, I would like to preface this with the power of words. I have learnt a powerful concept from one of the world's best Bible business coaches, Myron Golden. Myron uses King Solomons's Business Model to run his multimillion-dollar and multi-million impact business. I am a super fan, as you can tell. Anyways so it goes like this.

There are four levels of value in the world and the workplace; surprisingly, all are derived from God's creative blueprint. The four levels of value are **Implementation**, **unification**, **communication** and **imagination**.

The first level is the lowest level of value, and the last is the highest. As the name suggests, the first level is where you implement tasks and duties; the next level is where you delegate resources and people to do the tasks for you. In the third level of value , you use communication and words to give value; and lastly, lies the chief of the values; imagination, which is where ideas are born.

Sadly the worldly system teaches us and trains us to seek and strive for the lowest level of value of them all; the implementation level.

Schools, for example, were established to produce workers, i.e. implementers. Schools were never meant to produce creators and innovators. This is the reason why most creators and innovators usually drop out of school. School is not the ideal environment for imagination.

The world is happy when you can implement; doing some repetitive tasks in exchange for a paycheque. Implementation is easy to do but its the least rewarding, atleast to the person doing it. So we have people who would rather do that and only a few dare to level up to the real value that makes a difference.

They say actions speak louder than words, but in reality, words are more powerful than actions because words define all actions. In fact, given the order of the levels of value, I caution creators against commencing implementation before thorough imagination.

Actions must never travel faster than thoughts and words. The thoughts must always lead, as they are highest in value, then words, then connections, then actions.

Your body must never travel faster than your mind!

God doesn't have it backwards as humans do. God does not begin with implementation but with **imagination**. He imagines light as the solution to the void of darkness. Then he declares, " Let There Be Light."(communication) Then there is light.

Isn't it interesting too, that the most highly paid jobs in the world are those that revolve around imagination? Most people in Level 4 of value are the idea people. The ones who find ways to better everyone else's life. These are the dreamers who change the very structure of entire industries. These are people who think differently, like Steve Jobs. The keyword here is **think**.

Next to those who imagine are those who **communicate**, and that's exactly what God does next. He communicates. And God said. "Let there be Light . This is where the third principle of God's creative process takes over. You have to put your thoughts/ideas and imagination into words. Here is an important dynamic to understand, it doesn't matter how much the idea is worth or how great and high resolution the imagination is; it means nothing if it cannot be communicated. You see these levels of value are interconnected and interdependent. They serve each other.

The levels of value are so intricately connected that the successful transfer of value from one stage to another proves its legitimacy. So if an idea can not be communicated, it is enough proof that it's not worth implementing . For an idea to be effectively implemented, it must be communicated. God did not think anything into existence but He **spoke** things existence.

"By the word of the Lord were the heavens made; and all the host of them by the breath of His mouth." "For He spake,

and it was;" "He commanded, and it stood fast." Psalm 33:6,9.

God does not speak from spontaneousness; God is speaking from a grounded understanding of the void. God knows that the earth is without form and void. God has already figured out the necessary inspiration. God's speaking is an answer to the problem.

Speaking and communication are not on the third level of value by mistake. We use speech to communicate other values. The ability to speak, along with the capacity to imagine and generate ideas and solutions, is a divine trait.

It's one of those qualities we share with God but not with other creatures. Lions, for example, can roar, but they can't talk. Elephants can trumpet, but they can not speak. Chickens can cluck but cannot form intelligible speech. Only humans can speak, and that tells me that there's something unique and special about speaking, that it is a heavenly gift.

What is it exactly about speaking that is divine?

Speech, unlike imagination, **has the immediate ability to create**. The way speech creates is that it acts as a medium of transfer between the invisible and the visible. Speech lives on the boundary of imagination and materialization. It has both output and potential for input. Words therefore create.

And so we're told in proverbs. That

> *"Death and life are in the power of the tongue: and they that love it shall eat the fruit thereof." (Proverbs 18:21, KJV).*

Keeping this wisdom in mind, once you have found the inspiration and have gained a deep understanding of the void, you possess the ability to articulate and describe that void. This is where the transformative power of inspiration manifests, offering solutions to fill the void and bring about positive change. Words become the catalyst for turning inspiration into actionable plans and purposeful creation.

First, you have to put your thoughts and your inspiration into words. Then you have to communicate and declare your thoughts and intentions. Clarity has always been key from the first stage of this creative process. You have to be clear about the void and the missing thing in the marketplace. Creativity must have a purpose and direction. Any creation that humanity commences without a purpose always leads to destruction, no matter how noble it may seem otherwise. The purpose is what gives creation meaning.

You can't just create for the sake of it. You must be driven by purpose.

So, now you are clear about the void, you are clearly in touch with inspiration. Now, you have to clarify and communicate that in words. Write it down and make it clear. God says, let there be light. God does not say, let there be something that will compensate for the darkness or make things bright and make everything look amazing.

God doesn't use unnecessary adjectives and filler words. God is particular. You need the same specificity as a creator after God. For example, from my story, I discovered that the single most challenge creators face is lack of clarity and competence. That is the void, and because of spending time long enough on this issue, I got in touch with the inspiration to be able to create courses and partnerships that will help creators solve this problem. So I decided to write this book, among many other things. To support creators just like you.

I had to clarify the problem and write it down. I specified the problem, and because of that finding the solution became easier.

My solution ?

"Let there be NiyotheGreatest Media Agency(Studios)."

I'm not saying let there be something that will help creators. No, I am very specific. NiyotheGreatest Studios is the solution. It will provide you with the courses and resources you need to level up your creative career with clarity, confidence and competence.

Niyothegreatest Studios helps creators by providing the space and environment to create with clarity, confidence and competence through personalized, comprehensive coaching, courses, collaborations and connections with other like-minded creators to connect and co-create.

When you specify what you want, you will manifest it eventually, its a matter of time.

Jesus, in His ministry, would often approach sick people, and while He knew their conditions and limitations very well, He would still ask them,

"What do you want me to do for you?"

Even though it was clearly obvious that someone who is blind needs sight or someone who cannot walk wants the ability to walk, Jesus still sought their clarity and expression.

Why?

Because there is power in clarity, there is power in expression,and aticulation, there is power in speech. By making their desires known, they actively engaged in the process of receiving and manifesting their healing. When you verbalize your desires and needs, you give them form and substance. Your words hold weight and carry intention. Just as Jesus asked for explicit requests, you must also tap into the power of clarity and the spoken word to shape your reality.

So put your thoughts into words. You have been thinking a lot over the over years, you've been thinking of an idea, something you want to do, but it's not clear yet; write it down. Put it into words.

Communicating it is what will give it form and substance.Communicate it clearly and concisely, and you will be amazed at what you will create. Speaking it alone will create so much more than you can imagine. It's really already there because you have specified it.This is why I highly recommend that you write things down.

Next to speech, the other most powerful thing we can do as creators is to write. Writing is like thinking and speaking at the same time. It's what I call inaudible speech. But it goes directly to the mind. It forces you to imagine things and to get in touch with the creator of creativity.

Write down the solution you have for the problem you want to solve in detail

CHAPTER 6:
FEED BACK

"And God saw the light, that it was good" Genesis 1:4

I n the vast expanse of the universe, one of the most profound acts is the emergence of light from the omnipotent hands of the Creator. An event as magnificent as this, however, comes with an important lesson on feedback, particularly for creators. This chapter seeks to explore the power of feedback, both divine and human, and its implications for personal and collective growth.

Understanding the Feedback Principle

In the world of creativity and innovation, feedback is often considered a critical tool. It offers a glimpse into how our creations are perceived by the outside world. But what if feedback had a deeper, more profound meaning, one that resonated in the same way that the universe's first melodies did?

When God initiated light into existence, He didn't turn to external entities for validation. He, Himself, was the judge, and He declared it to be 'good'. This act of self-validation illuminates an essential principle for all creators: the power of introspective feedback.

Valuing Introspective Feedback

As creators, there is often an innate desire to seek validation from peers, mentors, or even the masses. However, as witnessed in the act of divine creation, the most vital feedback arises from within. Why?

You, as a creator, are privy to every nuance, every detail of your creation. You witness not just the final product but every thought, every process that led to its culmination.

Therefore, it becomes crucial to give oneself the credit due and recognize the value of what has been brought into existence. Not only should you celebrate your achievements, but also, adopt a reflective stance to gauge areas that might need enhancement.

Feedback isn't always rosy. Sometimes, it can be critical. The Bible provides a testament to this in Genesis 2:18. Even God, in His infinite wisdom, acknowledged a gap in His creation and identified the need for human companionship. It's a stark reminder that feedback isn't about criticism but about recognizing areas for growth and acting upon them.

> *"And the LORD God said, **It is not good** that the man should be alone; **I will make him an help meet for him**."*

To truly grasp the profoundness of feedback in Genesis 2:18, we must first delve into its context. After creating the heavens, the earth, and all living creatures, God formed Adam, the first man, from the dust. Placed in the Garden of Eden, Adam had the privilege of naming every creature. Yet, amidst this paradise and responsibility, there emerged a realization: no suitable helper was found for Adam.

Genesis 2:18 reads, "**And the Lord God said, 'It is not good for the**

man to be alone. I will make a helper suitable for him.'"

This statement from God stands out primarily because it marks a departure from the sequential affirmations throughout the creation account, where God sees His work and declares it "**good**."

God's observation here is twofold. First, He recognizes a deficiency — that man's solitude isn't ideal. Second, He outlines an intention to rectify this gap. Both elements are vital components of effective feedback.

The Implications of Constructive Feedback

The acknowledgment of Adam's solitude isn't a criticism of the initial creation but rather a recognition of an opportunity for enhancement. In doing so, God teaches us several essential aspects of feedback:

1. **Self-awareness**: Even the Divine, with limitless power and knowledge, reflects upon His work, demonstrating the importance of introspection and self-evaluation.

2. **Constructive Approach**: God doesn't merely identify a gap; He provides a solution. It's a lesson that feedback should always be forward-looking, paving the way for improvement.

3. **Acting on Feedback**: Not only does God acknowledge the need for human companionship, but He also acts on it by creating Eve. This emphasizes the essence of feedback: taking actionable steps.

God's introspection in Genesis 2:18 transcends the narrative of creation. It stands as a testament to the dynamic nature of life and projects. Nothing is so perfect that it cannot be improved upon. Recognizing gaps, even in divine creation, gives us a humbling perspective on our creations. We must be open to identifying areas of growth and, more importantly, acting upon them.

Genesis 2:18, though a simple verse, is laden with wisdom about the art and science of feedback. It isn't about criticism but about growth. It's about the courage to acknowledge gaps and the determination to bridge them. In this divine narrative, creators of all kinds can find inspiration to refine, evolve, and improve continuously.

The Pitfall of Perfectionism: A Deep Dive into Creative Evolution

The idea of perfection can be likened to a mirage in the desert — seemingly tangible yet forever elusive. As creators, the quest for perfection often seems like a noble pursuit. However, it can become an all-consuming obsession that blinds one to the real beauty and potential of their work. Every brushstroke, every note, every word is overanalyzed, seeking a state of faultlessness that may never be attained.

Vusi Tembekwayo on Perfectionism

Vusi Tembekwayo's perspective brings fresh air to the stifling room of perfectionism. His philosophy encourages a mindset shift. Instead of chasing an ever-elusive end state, why not embrace a dynamic process? This is the essence of his argument: perfection is a static goal, while improvement is dynamic, forever evolving and changing, much like life itself.

If perfection is the summit of a mountain, then improvement is the infinite sky above. While the summit offers a breathtaking view, it is finite. The sky, however, has no bounds. It's expansive and ever-changing. This analogy encapsulates the beauty of choosing continuous improvement over finite perfection.

As creators, every project, every piece, every creation is a step in this endless ascent. The moment you think you've reached the pinnacle is the very moment you might lose the enthusiasm and passion for further growth. This isn't a journey to a destination but rather an unending adventure.

God's act of creation, as detailed in holy scriptures, offers profound insights into this philosophy. Even in the divine act of creation, there wasn't an immediate state of perfection. Instead, there was evolution, adaptation, and improvement.

Day by day, the world took shape, each day building upon the previous. This methodical and phased creation emphasizes that even in divinity, there is a process, a journey, and an evolution. It wasn't about achieving perfection in an instant but about molding, refining, and perfecting over time.

In conclusion, the pitfall of perfectionism is that it seeks an end — a final state of flawlessness. However, in doing so, it limits the limitless, bounds the boundless. True creativity lies not in achieving a state of perfection but in the relentless pursuit of betterment.

Creators must learn to celebrate their achievements, no matter how small, while also recognizing that the journey is never over. This balance between acknowledgment and aspiration ensures a fulfilling creative process that continually strives for the infinite horizon of improvement.

Write down feedback on your business/ministry or brand

CHAPTER 7: THE PRINCIPLE OF DISTINCTION

"and God divided the light from the darkness." Genesis 1:4

I n the above-quoted scripture, we learn of a divine act where God divides the light from the darkness. He bestowed upon the light the name "day" and to the darkness, He named it "night." This act symbolizes the very genesis of differentiation and distinction. God, in His infinite wisdom, set light apart from darkness, highlighting the differences between what He brought forth and the pre-existing void. This principle of distinction holds profound significance not just in a theological or philosophical context but is deeply relevant to creators, entrepreneurs, and leaders from all walks of life, be it in business, ministry, religious institutions, or any other domain.

For anyone seeking success and meaningful impact, the lesson is clear: differentiation is key. Whether it's an idea, a product, a service, or a mission, it is imperative that it stands out, that it has its own identity. In a world overflowing with information and options, blending in is akin to invisibility. The most memorable and impactful entities are those that dare to be different, that carve their own path, and that offer something unique.

Therefore, as creators and innovators, it's essential to continuously ask oneself: "What sets my work apart?" "In what ways does it shine a light that contrasts with the prevailing darkness?" For just as God commenced His creation by establishing a clear distinction between day and night, so must we establish our ventures, projects, and endeavors with a distinct character and purpose to truly make a mark.

You are going nowhere if your work does not have a distinct voice, message, purpose, mission, and vision. If your book is not distinct enough, it won't sell. Distinction sets you apart and proves that you can actually deliver the value you promise to provide. So what is it that makes you distinct? What separates you from the rest of your peers and colleagues?

Besides ensuring capacity and authority, the principle of distinction also eliminates the need for competition. You are created uniquely and distinctly. You are **younique**. The psalmist says,

> *"I will praise thee; for I am fearfully and wonderfully made: Marvellous are thy works; And that my soul knoweth right well." Psalm 139:14 KJV.*

You are fearfully and wonderfully, distinctly made. No one person is exactly the same as you. No other person is exactly capable of the same things you are capable of.

In God's creative process, in God's kingdom there is no competition; there is no need for it. Competition comes from a place of lack and fear. Competition comes from lack of creativity and purpose. It is driven by laziness and covetousness.

Instead of competition, focus on **competence.** Competence in your field and domain of calling; focus on fulfilling the purpose God created you for. You are the only one that was created to fulfill it. You have your own fingerprint; In fact, you even have a unique voice print. All these are physical indications of the uniqueness that God has created you with.

In light of all this, it's about time we embrace our uniqueness. Appreciate and understand that you are fearfully and wonderfully made. That you're not here by chance or luck but that you are here for a reason, that there's a reason for your being, that you are here to fulfill and solve a specific problem, and that you have to deploy yourself into your space without fear.

People compete or compare themselves with other people because they lack the self-value and self-worth to understand that they are enough in themselves. They do not need another to validate or tell them who they are or what they are capable of; They only need to look to God, the only feedback that's acceptable and plausible.

When God created, He did not need anybody else's feedback because he is infinite without limitations. Unlike the human species, which is limited in every way. God is self-sustaining and omniscient without any dependencies. We, therefore, need that omniscient feedback from God. God must be able to see our work and say it is good.

This significantly elevates the value and vision of our work because now it has the signature of God himself—the one who created all things. And so we are told in the New Testament that whatever work we do, we should do it as if unto God.

> *"And whatsoever ye do, do it heartily, as to the Lord, and not unto men; knowing that of the Lord ye shall receive the reward of the inheritance: for ye serve the Lord Christ."Colossians 3:23-24 KJV*

It follows that for you to create a distinct product, business or brand, It begins with you recognizing your uniqueness in God. You have to embrace your uniqueness. You are so unique and distinct that if the kingdom of God loses you, it'll be a great loss. You are so unique that in the parable of the lost sheep. God is willing to deploy all his resources on one lost sheep, leaving the 99 sheep behind to go get the lost one.

In God's kingdom and economy, the principle and power of one runs through and through. One is enough in God's mind. Quality always precedes and supersedes quantity. If you were the only person on Earth, God would still deploy his resources to you because you uniquely reflect His image. There is no other James Niyomugabo. There will not be another NiyotheGreatest Studios; that's the uniqueness and the beauty of uniqueness. Competition crumbles to the dust, and collaboration compounds itself and grows. There is no comparison but complementing. Everything works together to Glorify God and make this world—a better place. So, be distinct.

Put a Name on It

As part of the distinguishing process, God calls the light day and the darkness he calls night. Now God goes into the business of naming. Naming is another interesting practice humans have adopted from none else but God himself. Naming is how you further make your work distinct and different. To distinguish it, you must name it, making it identifiable and findable. This is what God does.

As a creator, you must also be able to name your brand, put a name to your ideas and articulate your thoughts. If needs be patent your ideas. Clearly name the solution or the light, define the darkness or the problem, and put names to them.

This stage provides a whole new level of clarity to your creative process. You have specified the solution in terms of how it looks like. This could be a product requirement document specifying what needs to be created by product developers. For musicians, this could be the song's title, theme, and message they want to work on. Looks different for everyone. But the principle stays the same. Name it. For businesses, having a clear brand strategy and messaging will eventually solve the problem and the void they sense and see.

This naming also applies to the darkness; specify the area of your void you have explored and are committed to filling. Then name the place and the people that you have been sent to serve. What is your target audience? In detail, go over the demographics, geography, psychographics, interest and habits of the people in the void.

Naming represents ownership and overship(new word); you don't name things you don't own; you name things to prove that you own them and understand them in and out. And when you name them, you actually do.

Naming also demonstrates that you cherish the subjects of your designation. You don't assign names to things you don't hold dear; you name items that truly matter to you and whose significance you recognize. That's why, upon birth, we are given names to establish our uniqueness and identity early on. Just imagine if a child is born and not given a name. What would that signify? How would their life be? What about their sense of self? It would be overwhelmingly bewildering.

And yet, many of us have ideas and projects, even businesses, that we haven't given names to. Without names, they lack uniqueness, they lack form and structure and thus are void. To attain distinction, we must assign a name and be specific.

When it comes to branding, which is what naming is, we learn a myriad of principles from scripture, but I would be doing you a disservice if I didn't highlight this powerful biblical principle when it comes to branding and distinction. We learn this from

King Solomon. In King Solomon's business model and Brand strategy, we find a timeless strategy for all creators who what to excel and exceed.

In 1 Kings 1:10, the Queen of Sheba hears of the fame of Solomon and concerning the name of the Lord. This alone is fascinating enough, filled with divine creative revelation already. For example, we learn from this that King Solomon never necessarily deployed a marketing campaign to sell his business or brand. The success of King Solomon was mainly by word of mouth. This should shift your focus as a creator when you think of marketing and reaching the world.

What people call marketing today is not marketing; it's manipulation, coercion and infringement of privacy to steal information. Real marketing is word of mouth. In fact, in reality, major companies and brands agree.They understand that the real customers who stay are those who get convinced by word of mouth rather than those coerced through manipulative ads.

Enough with the marketing class.You know I never miss a teaching moment.

Continuing with the intriguing account of the Queen of Sheba's visit to King Solomon. She had heard of his fame, his unparalleled wisdom, and the magnificence of his kingdom. Yet, when she finally meets Solomon and witnesses his wisdom firsthand, she is overwhelmed. She says,

> *"It was a true report that I heard in mine own land of thy acts and of thy wisdom. Howbeit I believed not the words, until I came, and mine eyes had seen it: and, behold, the half was not told me: **thy wisdom and prosperity exceedeth the fame which I heard.**"* 1 Kings 10:7

When we hear the phrase, *"Your reputation precedes you,"* it's often an acknowledgment of someone's known abilities or accomplishments. But Solomon's interaction with the Queen of Sheba offers a potent revision: "**You must exceed your reputation.**"

Solomon's wisdom, the splendor of his court, and his prosperity were not just as the tales described; they were even more impressive. He personified the principle that to have sustainable success and lasting impact, one must consistently **outdo themselves**, surpassing not only others' expectations but also one's own.

The narrative of Solomon and the Queen of Sheba underscores the pivotal role of growth in achieving and maintaining success. The stagnation of abilities, knowledge, or character can lead to complacency, making one merely rest on their achievements. But Solomon's example reminds us that for sustainable success, growth is non-negotiable. You must continually refine, expand, and exceed your prior benchmarks.

Crafting a Distinction Statement: The Solomon Principle

The account of King Solomon and the Queen of Sheba from the Bible isn't just a tale of wisdom and prosperity; it provides a blueprint for individuals and brands striving for distinction in a saturated market. The core lesson? The power of surpassing reputation and cementing oneself as a paragon in a chosen domain.

At its heart, a distinction statement isn't a mere tagline or slogan. It is a crystallized representation of what you uniquely bring to the table. It articulates not only what you do but delves deep into the 'how' and 'why' behind your actions. The distinction statement offers a bird's-eye view of your brand's core, differentiating you from competitors and placing you on a pedestal of uniqueness.

Drawing from the story of Solomon, he wasn't merely another monarch on a throne. He stood as a beacon of wisdom, intelligence, and fair governance, characteristics that differentiated him from other rulers of his time. Visitors, like the Queen of Sheba, didn't just come to behold his wealth; they came to witness the profound wisdom and discernment that were synonymous with Solomon's name.

Constructing Your Statement

To craft a compelling distinction statement, introspection is paramount. Here's a step-by-step guide inspired by Solomon's example:

1. **Define Your Core**: Like Solomon's wisdom, pinpoint what lies at the heart of your brand or individuality. What is that one trait or service that stands out?

2. **Identify Your Audience**: Solomon's reign attracted the likes of the Queen of Sheba. Understand who is most likely to benefit from or be attracted to your core offering. Who are you speaking to?

3. **Delineate the Experience**: Describe the experience you offer. When visitors came to Solomon, they left in awe of his discernment. What emotions or reactions do you wish to evoke in those who encounter your brand or services?

4. **Be Authentic**: Solomon's reputation was not a mere embellishment; it was rooted in authenticity. Ensure your distinction statement isn't just a lofty promise but a genuine reflection of what you offer.

5. **Refinement and Evolution**: As times change and you grow, ensure that your distinction statement remains relevant. Continuously assess its alignment with your offerings and audience's needs, tweaking it for resonance.

In a world teeming with kings and queens, brands, and influencers, let your distinction statement be the shining crown that sets you apart. Like Solomon, ensure that when people encounter what you offer, they leave thinking, "Indeed, the half was not told me."

Conclusion: Beyond Fame and Into Legacy

While fame and reputation can open doors, it's the genuine substance behind that reputation that cements one's legacy. As creators, entrepreneurs, or individuals, the call is clear: strive to exceed, to grow, and to make a lasting impact. Let the tale of Solomon and the Queen of Sheba be a beacon, illuminating the path of excellence and the relentless pursuit of improvement.

Write down your distinction statement

CHAPTER 8:
LAUNCH DAILY

"And the evening and the morning were the first day." Genesis 1:5

Many people wonder why God took six literal days to create the entire world instead of doing it all in one single day. Some even question whether God was capable of creating everything in just a single click. However, the truth is that God had the power to do so but chose not to.

This decision was not due to any inability on His part but rather was a deliberate act with a purpose. By taking six days to create the world, God teaches us valuable lessons that are impossible to contain in a billion books. These lessons are essential for our personal growth and success. If we apply them to our lives, we will experience a level of success that we never thought possible.

The idea of God creating the entire universe in a single click is a fascinating and thought-provoking concept. However, upon closer examination, it becomes clear that such a notion would directly contradict the very principles of distinction and naming that underlie the creation of the universe.

If God were to create the entire cosmos in a single day, how could he possibly define and differentiate all of its various components? The universe is an impossibly vast and complex entity, containing countless planets, stars, and galaxies. To say "Let there be the universe" would be like saying "Let there be everything and nothing at the same time."

Instead, God approached the task of creation in a more deliberate and methodical way. He created individual components of the universe one by one.

Over time, these components came together to form the larger structures we see in the universe today. By taking this approach, God established and maintained the crucial principles of distinction and naming that are essential to the creation of any complex system.

And so following God's design and pattern I want you to now break down your big idea or business into parts and features.

To effectively bring your big idea or business to life, it's important to break it down into smaller parts and steps. For example, if you're creating a song, consider dividing it into stanzas. If you're working on building a relationship, try breaking it down into dates and focusing on each conversation individually. For your business, you might want to consider outlining your mission and goals, identifying your target clients, and developing effective strategies to achieve success. By breaking things down into manageable pieces, you can more easily identify areas for improvement and track your progress towards your ultimate goal.

You cannot create the ultimate void filler in one go. You cannot create a solution to an unspecified problem. That's really what it boils down to. We do not create for the sake of creating; remember, we only create because we are answering—a problem, limitation, or void.

And so we have to tackle this issue, one problem at a time.

Let's think of a product that helps entrepreneurs and personal brands run and launch their businesses confidently—taking care of all the documentation they need for smooth business operation.

That solution is a monolith. We have to break that down. Separate it into features. Into parts, into use cases and user stories. First of all, we have to feel the void. We have to feel the darkness. We have to understand what documentation emerging business owners need to launch and run their businesses. We need to answer, what is the void, why is the void, when is the void, and how is the void?

What is the void?

The void is that emerging businesses don't usually have the basics of how business works, so they need documentation that will clarify and simplify communication and increase clarity. The void exists when a business wants to be successful but has no vision, mission, brand or marketing strategy. This is void because it hinders growth and destroys confidence. The lack of clarity is the real problem that needs to be solved here.

Being an entrepreneur myself, I have experienced the hurdles of starting a business and chasing clarity. I know how much clarity can ensure that a business launches with confidence and competence.

So the solution I suggest for this problem is to provide services where I sit with business owners, one on one and go over the business model, brand strategy and marketing strategy to ensure that the business has enough clarity that can easily be communicated.

Breaking down the problem and solution into smaller parts is essential. It's impossible to create a polished final product in a single day.

To recap. First and foremost, you have to define the formlessness and void. Then you have to face it long enough to get inspiration, then get that inspiration into words, make sure your idea is unique and distinct and then reflect, reflect, reflect, feed back, feed back, feed back. And then get to the minimum viable product or solution.

You can't do everything in a single day. In God's creative process, we publish daily. God, deployed daily. You must be able to publish something new daily. At first glance, this concept feels a little too much, right? But if a day passes and you have not contributed anything to your journey, growth, and purpose, not even one inch, then something is wrong.

A thought-provoking quote states,

> *"If your today is the same as your yesterday, you have failed."*

This underscores the fundamental principle of growth. It's about continually striving to grow, expanding one's horizons, and essentially becoming more like God. Ponder upon the Creation, where God, in His boundless wisdom, infused value into the formless abyss. On the first day, He sculpted light, followed by shaping the skies, verdant landscapes, aquatic life, winged creatures, and the magnificent diversity of fauna on subsequent days.

The crowning work of his creation was humanity. Created on day number 6. This illustrates the essence of progressively building something valuable and beloved. Like God's methodical creation, it is imperative to focus on developing a functional Minimum Viable Product/solution (MVP/S) that garners affection and resonates with those it serves.

Here's a quick lesson from this. Even though you can't create a finished product in a day, you don't have to finish in order to deploy. And many people make this mistake, especially content creators and business owners. They think that before starting a business, launching, or going into the world, they must first become perfect and figure everything out.

First of all, that's impossible because even after five years into your business, you will still have to make some adjustments; five years in your band, you still have to adapt; five years in your relationship, you still have to finetune. What you need is a minimum viable, lovable product or solution, not necessarily a finished product/solution. So when God created light, he was done. The only qualification for your minimum viable value is that it has to be targeting a specific use case.

So God was certain that the light solved the darkness problem. And he did not need to worry about that anymore because now the solution exists; now we have a solution to the problem; therefore, we can deploy it, and people can start using it.

When God created vegetation, he was done. He deployed. After that, God created animals and fish in the sea; he was done. He deployed. And that's the same spirit we need to have. So what's your minimum viable value? It could be a business idea that you have had for a long time. Do you want to start a business that helps people make money; you have a business that teaches people how to do software development. Oh, you have a product that teaches people how to make music. You don't have to complete it before you can release it.

By design, God's creative strategy is agile. In software development, there is a concept known as Agile Development. Although it's mostly used in software, it's an approach that can be customized to all creative enterprises.

Agile development refers to a dynamic and iterative approach to software development that emphasizes flexibility, collaboration, and customer satisfaction. Rather than following a linear path, Agile breaks the development process into smaller, manageable pieces called iterations.

Each iteration is like a mini-project in itself, encompassing design, coding, testing, and review. This method enables teams to be more responsive to changes and customer feedback, as they can easily adapt and make improvements along the way.

Collaboration is key in Agile development, with ongoing communication between cross-functional teams and stakeholders. By focusing on delivering a functional product in incremental stages, Agile aims to provide high-quality software that aligns with customer needs and expectations while also allowing for rapid adaptation to any changes or new requirements that may arise during the development process

The cool thing about a minimum viable product is that you can continuously improve it, reflect and repeat the process once you have the minimum functional product or value. I'll give an example. So on day one, God creates light. But on day four, he goes deeper into photography. And he creates the sun, the moon, and the stars. You see where I'm going?

Publish Daily

If you think about the principle of launching daily in the context of content creators, a wonderful and massive opportunity is unearthed. The imperative is straightforward. Post daily!

Now at first, this sounds like a daunting task, but trust me its benefits outway any doubt or dauntyness you may feel. Publishing or posting daily is a necessity for creators; while this may look different for everybody, allow me to make the general exemplification.

Most creators that I know, and by no doubt including you, want to, in their own words, "**change the world**". Now that's a bold claim, and well and good. Boldness and confidence must be encouraged at all levels, after all it's the image of God to be bold.

But here is the problem; How do you expect to change the world with a single post a week or a single post a month? How is that going to happen? How can you make any real impact in an over-saturated world and marketplace if you are seldom visible or influential?

The point? Without any judgment by the way,

Posting or publishing daily is not a privilege or nicety; it's a necessity if you want to make a real impact and change in this world, be it physical or digital. The reason for this is that posting daily or the equivalence thereof introduces undeniable **omnipresence**, making you and your work ubiquitous and consequently magnifying your influence and impact.

Something you can use to achieve omnipresence on social media and, by default, the real world is repurposing, something we wil dive deeper into in chapter 10, for now, launch, deploy, export, share, and sell.

Launch your minimum viable product/solution, post daily, publish daily and make sure your work is out there for people to see.To achieve your finished product, it's important to complete a minimum amount of work every day. This may vary depending on your situation, but the key is to ensure that tasks are moved from the backlog to the "done" column on a daily basis. This will help you stay on track and make progress towards your goal.

So what are you publishing today?

CHAPTER 9:
DELEGATION

"And God said, Let the earth bring forth grass..." Genesis 1:11

Another powerful principle to consider when creating is the principle of delegation. Something we touched upon briefly in the four levels of value. The second level of value is unification, which can simply be summarized as delegating resources to get things done(implementation). The four levels of value did not create themselves, God created them, and that's why we find them rooted and seated in the book of Genesis.

When God created at first, He said let there be light, and there was light. So God speaks into nothingness and the darkness and the void—something you should do as a creator. Don't waste your time if you can't speak to the void. Anyways I digress.

On day number two, God creates the sky and land. On the third day God creates vegetation. The way He does it is different from how He created on the first day. God speaks to the land to bring forth vegetation.. This is delegation 101.

God no longer has to say, let there be vegetation, but God being judicial with his resources uses what he's already created to create more. You get the drift right? T

Therefore, when you create things in your own creative space, you need to understand that your creation is an agent in your creation. More than the delegation of resources , there is also delegation of human resource.

Delegation involves communicating with people, building a team, and understanding that you cannot do everything independently. You need resources (Human/natural resources) to fulfill the goal and the dream that you have. So be willing to delegate. Those who delegate are those who succeed. In fact, If you think of all the successful people in this world, you will find that they delegate daily.

The Principle of Delegation in Genesis: Orchestrating Creation through Shared Responsibility

Genesis begins with the grandeur of God's creative power, bringing forth the heavens, the earth, and all living beings. Amid this expanse of life, God created humanity, bestowing upon them a unique role. In Genesis 1:28, God commands Adam and Eve,

> *"Be fruitful and multiply, and fill the earth and subdue it; and have dominion over the fish of the sea, and over the birds of the air, and over every living thing that moves upon the earth."*

This command is not just a blessing but a delegation of authority.

In entrusting humans with the responsibility of stewardship over all creation, God was delegating a significant portion of His authority on Earth to mankind. Humans were not just passive inhabitants; they were active stewards, expected to take on the role of caretakers and overseers. This divine trust signifies the essence of delegation: entrusting responsibility not just to offload tasks but to empower and uplift the potential of those to whom the tasks are delegated.

The principle of delegation found in Genesis teaches that true leadership isn't about holding onto power but distributing it. It's about recognizing the potential in others and giving them the space, authority, and responsibility to flourish. God, in His infinite wisdom, understood that the Earth would thrive not just by His direct intervention but through the shared responsibility He bestowed upon humanity.

Furthermore, Adam's task of naming the animals showcases another layer of this principle. Naming, in ancient cultures, often denoted understanding and authority. By allowing Adam, to name the animals, God was delegating a portion of His creative authority, enabling Adam to participate actively in the order and structure of creation.

This timeless lesson from Genesis offers a blueprint for contemporary leadership. Effective leaders, like the divine example set before them, recognize the value of delegation. They understand that sharing responsibility fosters growth, innovation, and a collective sense of purpose. As God entrusted humanity with the Earth, so should leaders entrust their teams with meaningful responsibilities, nurturing an environment where each individual's potential can truly unfold.

Other examples of delegation in the Bible include

Moses and Jethro:

In Exodus 18, Moses' father-in-law, Jethro, observed that Moses was wearing himself out by personally judging the disputes of all the Israelites. Jethro advised him to delegate these duties by appointing capable leaders over thousands, hundreds, fifties, and tens. Only the most difficult cases would come to Moses, while simpler disputes would be resolved by these leaders. Heeding this advice, Moses efficiently managed the needs of an entire nation.

The Twelve Apostles:

In Acts 6:1-4, as the early Christian church grew, the twelve apostles found themselves unable to attend to both their prayer and ministry of the word and the daily distribution of food to the widows. They delegated the responsibility of food distribution to seven men, allowing the apostles to focus on prayer and preaching. This act of delegation not only ensured that the community's needs were met but also allowed the gospel to spread more efficiently.

King Solomon:

Solomon, renowned for his wisdom, effectively managed the Kingdom of Israel by delegating responsibilities. He appointed twelve officers, each responsible for supplying provisions to the palace for one month a year (1 Kings 4:7-19). This system ensured a consistent supply without overburdening any single region.

King David and the Levites:

In 1 Chronicles 23-26, King David organized the Levites, priests, and musicians into specific roles and tasks for the service of the Temple. He delegated specific duties, ensuring orderly worship and proper care and maintenance of the sanctuary.

Nehemiah:

Tasked with rebuilding the walls of Jerusalem, Nehemiah faced opposition and challenges. Instead of trying to oversee every part of the project himself, Nehemiah delegated sections of the wall to different families and groups. This collective effort, as detailed in Nehemiah 3, allowed for the wall's efficient reconstruction.

The practical steps that can be derived from these biblical examples underscore the importance of delegation in leadership and creative pursuits. For modern creators and leaders, these stories provide valuable lessons that can be adapted to today's fast-paced and interconnected world:

1. **Recognize the Limits of Individual Capacity:** Just as Moses realized he couldn't judge every dispute by himself, creators should understand that trying to handle all aspects of a project single-handedly can lead to burnout. Recognizing one's limitations is the first step toward effective delegation.

2. **Identify and Appoint Qualified Individuals**: Moses, the apostles, Solomon, and David chose individuals with specific skills and attributes to carry out certain tasks. Similarly, creators should identify team members or collaborators who possess the required expertise or skills to handle specific tasks.

3. **Provide Clear Instructions and Expectations**: Clearly define the roles and responsibilities for those you're delegating tasks to. This clarity ensures that everyone understands their duties, as seen in the precise roles allocated by David for the Temple's service.

4. **Create Systems and Structures**: King Solomon's approach to provisioning his palace is an excellent example of creating a system. He divided the responsibility among twelve officers, ensuring consistency. In modern terms, this could mean setting up workflows, using project management tools, or establishing routines.

5. **Monitor Progress and Provide Feedback**: Nehemiah didn't just assign tasks and walk away; he kept a close eye on the progress of the wall's construction. Periodically check in on projects, provide feedback, and make necessary adjustments.

6. **Empower and Trust Your Delegates**: Once you've entrusted a task to someone, give them the autonomy and trust to complete it. Jethro advised Moses to handle only the most challenging cases, implying that he should trust his appointed leaders to manage the simpler disputes.

7. **Regularly Re-evaluate and Adjust**: The early Christian church's growth meant that the apostles needed to reassess and adjust their roles, leading to the appointment of the seven men. As projects evolve or as businesses grow, creators should regularly re-evaluate their delegation strategies.

8. **Celebrate Collective Achievements**: Acknowledging the contributions of all involved fosters a positive and collaborative environment. Just as the collective effort in Nehemiah's story

led to the successful reconstruction of the wall, recognizing team achievements can boost morale and encourage further collaboration.

9. **Prioritize and Delegate Accordingly**: The apostles chose to focus on prayer and preaching and delegated food distribution. For creators, this means prioritizing tasks that align most closely with their core objectives and delegating other responsibilities.

10. **Provide Resources and Training**: Ensure that those you delegate tasks to have the necessary resources and training to succeed. This not only empowers them but also ensures the quality and efficiency of the work.

Effective delegation is a crucial skill for creators and leaders. By understanding its importance and implementing these practical steps derived from biblical examples, they can optimize their efforts, avoid burnout, and achieve their goals more efficiently.

Delegation: A Divine Mandate

Delegation stands as a testament to the divine strategy, one that even the Almighty employs and values. It operates on a principle more profound than merely sharing authority. At its core, delegation is about service—serving and uplifting those around you. By delegating, you are not just passing on a task; you're sharing a vision, expanding its horizons beyond the limitations of a single mind. This sharing process inherently shifts the focus from an individual to the collective, fostering a sense of unity and shared purpose.

There's an adage that if you want to soar higher, you need to hire. This principle is vividly illustrated by Rabbi Lapin in his enlightening book, "Business Secrets from the Bible: Spiritual Success Strategies for Financial Abundance." Rabbi Lapin highlights a key aspect of the Jewish approach to life and business: the value of delegation over the pride of self-sufficiency. Instead of striving to handle every chore personally in the name of saving money, the emphasis is on delegating tasks. This approach not only ensures tasks are expertly handled by those specialized in them but also frees one up to focus on life's higher callings and more significant pursuits. As Rabbi Lapin notes, it's uncommon to find a Jew washing their car or roofing their own house. They recognize the wisdom in entrusting such tasks to others, thus providing opportunities for many while simultaneously freeing themselves to concentrate on more crucial matters.

Expanding on this principle, it becomes evident that God's blessings flows more abundantly when our actions benefit a broader community rather than just ourselves. Consider two projects: one solely enriching you and another that creates opportunities and prosperity for dozens, hundreds or thousands of other people. Which do you think aligns more with the divine plan?Which do you think God will be interested in? Which venture is more likely to earn God's favor?

When one chooses the path of delegation and collaborative effort, they not only enrich their ventures but also create ripples of opportunities and blessings for many. Thus, it might be surmised that God finds more incentive to bless collective efforts over solitary endeavours. The thought is compelling: perhaps the more we extend opportunities to others, the more we align with the divine blueprint for shared prosperity. Let's ponder that profound notion.

Let's take delegation a step further. In line with the principle of delegation, God uses what he has already created to create something else.He speaks to the land to bring forth vegetation, then he speaks to the sea to bring forth the fishes and the firmament to bring birds, but on day six, when he creates man, a dramatic change and shift occurs. God does not speak to the sea, land, or nothingness anymore. He speaks to Himself. This transition is one worthy of study and consideration. Why does God speak to himself when he comes to creating humanity?

In your creative journey, you will have to speak to various places, spaces, and people, but to get to your finished product;

you must now speak to yourself. Its not enough to just create a product or a brand that speaks to the various situations. You have to create something in your own image. Something that has your signature? Something that reflects you.

And this is, by default, what ends up happening anyways because every product reflects the team that built it. Every solution, product, content, and idea Is a reflection of the person/team who built it. For you to reach that zone where you have something that reflects you fully, you can't rely on speaking to nothingness; you can't depend on speaking to places and spaces. You now have to speak to yourself/your team and say let's make something in our image.

Let us do something that reflects us. The cool thing about branding, too, is that whatever product you create, whatever idea you make, whatever organization is established, although you are looking to spaces, speaking to places and speaking to yourself, it has to be something that is beyond you.

An image that is not greater than yourself, a brand that is not bigger than yourself, is not worth creating. You have to focus on creating something that will outlive you. This is why delegation is so important. If your idea dies with your death. It means you have not executed the idea the right way.

The idea, business, brand and or product should be able to continue even after you are gone. Remember, it's a void you are filling, and the void you are filling was not and is not your satisfaction. Although that may come about as a by-product but that's not why you create. We don't create to be fulfilled; we create to fulfill.

And until that void is filled, our work is not done, meaning our death should not be the predictor nor indicator of our success. Our goal and our vision must not pass away when we do.

Write down to whom you must delegate to ensure your creation is successful and outlives you.

CHAPTER 10. BE FRUITFUL AND MULTIPLY

"And God blessed them, and God said unto them, Be fruitful, and multiply, and replenish the earth, and subdue it: and have dominion over the fish of the sea, and over the fowl of the air, and over every living thing that moveth upon the earth." - Genesis 1:28

The book of Genesis, the first chapter of the Bible, is not just an account of creation—it's a testament to the principle of multiplication. When Adam and Eve were formed, they were not just created to exist; they were crafted with a purpose. The Almighty didn't mince His words, "Be fruitful, and multiply, and replenish the earth, and subdue it: and have dominion over every living thing." (Genesis 1:28, KJV)

In essence, they were given the authority and the command to increase, to spread, and to rule. This is the earliest indicator of God's design for growth and multiplication, a principle deeply ingrained in the fabric of creation.

The Vine and The Branches: A Reminder through Christ

Centuries later, Jesus, through his teachings, re-emphasizes the value of being fruitful. In John 15:5, He uses the metaphor of a vine, stating,

"I am the vine; ye are the branches: He that abideth in me, and I in him, the same bringeth forth much fruit: for without me ye can do nothing."

This metaphor drives home the point that any endeavour outside of God's will and presence is futile.

For modern-day creators, entrepreneurs, and business owners, this serves as a reminder: your ventures and ideas will only bear fruit, multiply, and prosper when they are aligned with a higher purpose, when they are connected to the Vine.

Delving deeper into the metaphor, the relationship between the vine and the branches offers profound insights into the intricate balance of dependency and autonomy. A branch, though individual in its bearing, draws its nourishment and strength from the vine. Cut off from the vine, the branch withers and dies. This underscores the pivotal role the Source, in this context, God, plays in the thriving of any endeavor. Even as entrepreneurs champion the virtues of self-reliance and autonomy, the parable serves as a gentle reminder that true, sustained success is rooted in a deeper, divine connection.

Furthermore, this interdependence paints a broader picture of creation and purpose. The vine doesn't exist merely to support the branches, nor do the branches exist in isolation. They coalesce to form a living entity, each part integral to the whole's wellbeing.

Similarly, our individual ventures and creations aren't just about personal gain or acclaim. They're cogs in a grand cosmic design, and when they resonate with this greater purpose, the results are exponential. Businesses prosper, ideas spread, and creations inspire when they are attuned to this harmonious symphony of existence.

For the modern creator, the vine and branches analogy isn't just spiritual; it's a tangible blueprint for success. Just as the health of a branch is inextricably linked to its connection to the vine, the prosperity of a venture is tethered to its alignment with core principles and values. In a world brimming with fleeting trends and transient success stories, the timeless wisdom Christ imparted serves as an anchor. As we navigate the challenging terrains of business, innovation, and creativity, may we constantly seek alignment, drawing sustenance from the Vine, and in doing so, cultivate ventures that are not just successful but also significant.

God's design for multiplication is evident in every facet of nature. Consider vegetation. Trees bear fruit containing seeds, and these seeds, when planted, can produce more trees. This continuous cycle is not just multiplication; it's exponential growth. Genesis 1:11 says,

> "And God said, Let the earth bring forth grass, the herb yielding seed, and the fruit tree yielding fruit after his kind, whose seed is in itself, upon the earth: and it was so."

This principle, where each creation contains within it the ability to recreate and multiply, is a testimony to God's ingenious design.

Challenging Modern Notions: The Biblical Perspective on Wealth and Growth

Navigating through the convoluted narratives of our modern era, especially within certain Christian circles, it becomes evident that there's a burgeoning tension between perceptions of wealth and the essence of piety. A predominant notion, sadly misconstrued, is that true piety is synonymous with poverty while affluence is painted with a broad brush of skepticism and, sometimes, derision. However, this binary interpretation is an oversimplification and, more crucially, isn't in congruence with the overarching messages of the Bible.

The Scriptures, particularly in the foundational chapters of Genesis, echo a divine imperative: "**Be fruitful and multiply.**" While the immediate connotation might be procreation, a deeper dive into biblical texts suggests that this command extends beyond mere reproduction. It's an exhortation towards prosperity, growth, and the expansion of God's Kingdom on Earth. And this prosperity isn't restricted to spiritual riches alone; it encompasses our personal, communal, and even financial well-being.

In Proverbs 10:22, it's written,

> *"The blessing of the LORD brings wealth, without painful toil for it."*

Here, the Bible acknowledges wealth as a blessing, not a curse. The Psalms are replete with verses celebrating God's provision and abundance. Thus, the vilification of wealth as inherently corrupt or contrary to Christian values is not only a misrepresentation but also denies believers the fullness of life God intends for them.

However, the Bible also offers a balanced perspective. While it champions prosperity, it does so with an emphasis on righteousness, justice, and charity. Wealth, in the biblical sense, isn't a hoarding of resources but a tool for stewardship, benevolence, and the betterment of society.

As with most divine principles, there's a caveat, a test of faith and resilience. The prosperity that the Scriptures advocate doesn't come on a silver platter. Just as the seed must relinquish its current form, be buried, and undergo transformation before it blossoms into a plant, individuals and communities desiring growth must embrace sacrifice. This sacrifice could manifest in various forms: hard work, patience, deferred gratification, or even weathering criticism. The analogy of the seed is profoundly allegorical. It signifies that in the realms of business, personal growth, or creativity, true success emerges from moments of surrender, metamorphosis, and perseverance.

Furthermore, this principle is not solely restricted to the tangible; it's equally applicable in the spiritual realm. Growth in faith, too, demands sacrifices – be it in the form of time dedicated to prayer, acts of service, or even periods of waiting and seeking.

In summary it's vital to realign modern notions of wealth and growth with the holistic biblical perspective. While the Scriptures indeed encourage prosperity, they do so with an emphasis on righteousness, humility, and the greater good. Embracing this balanced view allows believers to live in the fullness of God's blessings while being agents of positive change in the world.

The Modern Pursuit of Multiplication and Its Limitations

The entrepreneurial realm, with its rapidly evolving dynamics and constant push for innovation, has indeed stumbled upon certain principles that echo ancient wisdom. Among these insights is the recognition of the power of multiplication as a force to propel success to unparalleled heights. Grant Cardone's 10X Rule stands as a testament to this awareness. By urging individuals to set goals that are tenfold of their initial estimates and to take actions tenfold more than their preliminary plans, Cardone encapsulates the spirit of expansive thinking and aggressive action.

However, while the 10X mindset certainly stands out against the backdrop of mediocrity and complacency, it is still, perhaps unknowingly, tethered to human-imposed limitations. This is not a critique of Cardone's philosophy but rather an observation that even in our most audacious pursuits, we might still be scratching merely the surface of what's possible.

Turning to ancient scriptures, we encounter a more radical approach to multiplication in the teachings of Jesus. Through the parable of the sower, He paints a vivid picture of varying levels of abundance. The yields described are not just tenfold but extend to 30-fold, 60-fold, and even an astounding 100-fold. These numbers are not arbitrary; they represent the boundless possibilities that arise when one aligns with divine principles and operates from a space of faith and purpose.

To the modern creator and entrepreneur, these figures offer more than just quantitative benchmarks. They beckon us to a realm where conventional logic takes a backseat, and divine multiplication directs the course. It's a realm where the barriers of what's deemed 'possible' are continually recalibrated, pushing us to think, dream, and act in ways that transcend our self-imposed boundaries.

In essence, while contemporary entrepreneurial wisdom, like the 10X Rule, offers a significant leap from the norm, the true challenge lies in whether we are willing to go even further. Are we prepared to embrace the 30x, 60x, or 100x mindset? Can we position ourselves in the vast expanse between our greatest imaginations and divine potential?

In this expansive space, creators are called not merely to multiply but to do so in alignment with a higher purpose. It's not just about bigger numbers but about the quality of impact, depth of influence, and alignment with a purpose that transcends fleeting market trends. As modern creators, our pursuit shouldn't merely be about multiplication for the sake of growth but about resonating with a deeper, more purposeful form of expansion, one that is truly in line with the divine blueprint of multiplication.

The Pain & Reward of Multiplication

The pursuit of multiplication, be it in personal growth, business expansion, or the realization of creative potential, is intrinsically tied to a sequence of trials, transformations, and triumphs. While this journey promises great rewards, it is not for the faint of heart. It demands resilience, perseverance, and an unwavering commitment to the end goal.

Drawing parallels with the biblical narrative, we're reminded of the transition of childbirth from a harmonious process in Eden to one marked by pain and labour post the fall of Adam and Eve. This profound shift illustrates a fundamental truth about our human experience: value and victory often emerge from the crucible of challenge.

In the realm of business and creation, this is manifested in numerous ways. Entrepreneurs often face moments of doubt, financial constraints, market fluctuations, and even personal crises. For artists and creators, there's the battle with the blank canvas, writer's block, public critique, and the pressure of originality. However, these tribulations, while formidable, are not the end but merely the chiselling forces shaping the masterpiece.

It's essential to perceive these challenges not as deterrents but as essential components of the multiplication process. Just as a seed must endure the darkness and pressure of the soil to sprout and thrive, our ventures and visions must navigate adversity to flourish truly.

But why endure all this pain? Why face these trials?

The answer lies in the unparalleled joy and satisfaction that ensues. To witness an idea transform into reality, to see a venture impact lives, or to experience personal growth that once seemed impossible – these are the rewards of enduring the journey of multiplication. They provide a sense of purpose, accomplishment, and legacy that far outweighs the initial struggles.

Moreover, the hurdles themselves, in retrospect, become valuable lessons. They hone our skills, refine our strategies, and deepen our understanding, equipping us for even greater challenges and subsequent successes. Without them, our victories might seem hollow, devoid of the richness that comes from overcoming.

In conclusion, while the path of multiplication is strewn with challenges, it is these very challenges that lend depth, value, and meaning to our pursuits. As we embrace this journey with all its highs and lows, we not only achieve our goals but also evolve, transforming into versions of ourselves that are stronger, wiser, and more resilient. In the dance between pain and reward, lies the true essence of growth and multiplication.

One of the most direct and profound ways you can multiply as a creator is through repurposing. Repurposing means taking one thing that was meant for an initial use and then reusing it again for another use, obtaining different results and serving different purposes using the same or derivative of the same object or product.

The concept of repurposing can be seen a lot in scripture but for the sake of time let us restrict ourselves to Genesis 1 and 2, where our blueprint gails from.

1. **The Duality of Light and Darkness**:

"In the beginning God created the heaven and the earth... And God said, Let there be light: and there was light. And God saw the light, that it was good: and God divided the light from the darkness. And God called the light Day, and the darkness he called Night." (Genesis 1:1,3-5) Here, a single act of creation — ushering forth light — served dual purposes. The light did not only dispel the primordial darkness but also marked the beginning of time, segmenting it into 'day' and 'night'. One act, multiple outcomes.

2. **The Firmament's Dual Role**:

"And God said, Let there be a firmament in the midst of the waters, and let it divide the waters from the waters... And God called the firmament Heaven." (Genesis 1:6-8) The firmament, or Heaven, divided the waters, but it wasn't solely a partition. This expanse later became the realm where birds would "fly above the earth in the open firmament of heaven" (Genesis 1:20). The same creation, initially a boundary, assumed another purpose as the domain for winged creatures.

3. **Land, the Repurposed Earth**:

"And God said, Let the waters under the heaven be gathered together unto one place, and let the dry land appear: and it was so." (Genesis 1:9) What was once submerged became the land, a hospitable territory for diverse life forms. This repurposing of the earth ensured the subsequent emergence of flora and fauna, turning it into a cradle of life.

4. **Vegetation's Recursive Purpose**:

"And God said, Let the earth bring forth grass, the herb yielding seed... and it was so." (Genesis 1:11) The vegetation wasn't merely a static creation. It was designed to yield seed, ensuring the perpetuation of plant life. Through the act of bearing seeds, plants were in essence repurposed to be both sustenance and the means for future sustenance.

5. **Humanity's Expanding Roles**:

"Then God said, Let us make man in our image, after our likeness: and let them have dominion... over all the earth... And the Lord God took the man, and put him into the Garden of Eden to dress it and to keep it." (Genesis 1:26; 2:15) Man, initially created as the steward of Earth's creatures, was later repurposed to tend and cultivate the Garden, showcasing the adaptability and multiplicity of human purpose.

6. **The Sanctification of the Seventh Day**:

"And on the seventh day God ended his work which he had made; and he rested on the seventh day from all his work which he had made. And God blessed the seventh day, and sanctified it." (Genesis 2:2-3) While initially just another day in the span of time, the seventh day was repurposed to be a beacon of rest and spiritual reflection, differentiating it from the other days.

The narrative of creation in Genesis underscores God's mastery in maximizing value and utility. Every element woven into the fabric of existence holds multiple, interconnected purposes. For modern creators, this is an inspiration to ensure their creations are not just innovative but versatile, echoing the Divine practice of repurposing.

Multiplication: A Desire Rooted in Omnipresence

Throughout history, humanity has been driven by an innate desire to multiply, not just in terms of population but in all aspects of life. This concept isn't solely based on numerical increase or reproduction; it transcends to a deeper spiritual and philosophical realm. The urge to multiply can be perceived as an echo of the omnipresence of a higher power or God. When we speak of God in many religious and philosophical teachings, omnipresence stands out as a fundamental attribute. This means that God is everywhere, aware of all things, and present in all moments. In this light, humanity's drive to multiply can be seen as an aspiration to mirror this divine trait.

The very act of multiplication enables humans to have a representation of themselves everywhere. From ancient civilizations that left their marks through sprawling cities and art to today's generation that leaves digital footprints, the goal has always been the same: a persistent and widespread presence. Just as art, literature, and now social media profiles serve as our representations, multiplying ensures that a part of us, our beliefs, our legacies, and our genes continue to exist across different locations and even timelines.

This desire to be "everywhere" isn't merely about ego or the quest for immortality. It's a deep-seated yearning to be connected to the vastness of the universe, to have an influence and resonance beyond our immediate surroundings. Every time humans have tried to expand their territories, influence, or even their knowledge, there is an underlying desire to be more connected to the broader universe and to emulate the omnipresent nature of God.

And it's not just about physical or tangible multiplication. Our wish to spread ideas, to share stories, and influence thoughts are all derivatives of the same desire. Religions have spread, philosophies have traversed continents, and stories have been passed down through generations. Every time a concept or belief becomes widespread, it's humanity's way of marking its omnipresent aspirations. The beauty of this is that it's not about conquering or domination but a testament to our innate need to be recognized, understood, and felt universally.

In conclusion, the act and desire of multiplication is a profound aspect of human nature. It can be considered as an echo or reflection of our aspiration to resemble the omnipresence of God. By seeking to have a representation of ourselves everywhere, we aim for a universal connection, tapping into a desire that's both spiritual and profoundly human.

The Power of Repurposing: A Comprehensive Guide with an Action Plan

Omnipresence isn't just about being everywhere but making sure your content is impactful, relevant, and dynamic across platforms. This involves understanding two key concepts: Batch Production and Repurposing.

Understanding the Concepts:

1. **Batch Production**: Producing content en masse or in large quantities at once. This aids in consistency, allowing creators to have a reservoir of content to pull from.

2. **Repurposing**: The art of taking existing content and reshaping it into various formats to suit different platforms or audiences.

The Beauty of Content Longevity:

Content has a shelf life longer than we often realize. That insightful video you made five years ago? It still holds potential.

The trick lies in presenting it in a refreshed, relevant manner.

Action Plan: Unlocking the Power of Repurposing

1. **Audit Your Existing Content**:

- Go through your archives. Identify content that performed well or holds evergreen value.

- Tag or categorize content based on themes, insights, or relevance to make it easier to repurpose later.

2. **Decide on New Formats**:

- Identify where your audience spends their time. Are they on blogs? Podcasts? Social media shorts?

- Match your audited content to these formats. A video could become a blog. A series of blogs could turn into a book.

3. **Redesign and Adapt**:

- For videos, consider trimming, adding updated graphics, or using snippets for shorter formats like social media stories.

- For written content, look at changing the tone, updating statistics, or reformatting for different platforms.

4. **Optimize for Each Platform**:

- Remember, each platform has its unique audience. Adjust your content to cater to the preferences of each. For instance, LinkedIn might prefer more professional tones, while Instagram might favor casual, visual content.

5. **Plan a Release Schedule**:

- Consistency is key. Use tools like content calendars to schedule and release your repurposed content.

- Ensure you're not over-saturating any one platform.

6. **Engage and Interact**:

- Repurposing is not just about re-releasing. Engage with your audience, gather feedback, and iterate.

- This engagement can also give insights into what other content they might want to see repurposed.

7. **Evaluate and Adjust**:

- Keep track of performance metrics. Some content might perform well in one format but not another.

- Adjust your strategy accordingly. Consider new platforms, trends, and audience preferences.

Repurposing content isn't just about maximizing output; it's about maximizing impact. With the right strategy, one piece of content can ripple across the digital sphere in multiple forms, ensuring that your message reaches and resonates with as many people as possible. Embrace the power of repurposing and unlock a world of omnipresence in your digital space.

A Clarion Call to Dominion and Legacy

Every epoch of history has its game-changers, its luminaries who redefine paradigms and recalibrate the scales of what's possible. To you, the creator, the visionary entrepreneur, the purpose-driven business owner – the baton has been handed. The mandate is unmistakable: Arise, multiply, and exert dominion. But this dominion isn't a mere assertion of power; it's a harmonious blend of responsibility, influence, and intentional impact.

Operating within your niche or sector isn't just about turning a profit or gaining traction. It's about imprinting a legacy, etching your signature on the annals of time. The onus is on you not to just be a passive participant but to be a beacon of change, illuminating the voids and dispelling the prevailing darkness. This is not just a pursuit; it's a spiritual mission, echoed aptly in 2 Corinthians 10:5. Here, we are reminded to actively rebuff any thought or imagination that runs counter to the divine blueprint, to anchor every ambition in alignment with God's grand design.

The book of Genesis isn't just an account of beginnings; it's a treasure trove of principles, laden with nuggets of wisdom that can steer your enterprise towards unprecedented success. These aren't mere words; they are divinely inspired strategies that have stood the test of time. The metaphor of the Vine, as elucidated in John 15:5, reinforces this. Our potency isn't birthed from isolated endeavours but is amplified when we remain inextricably linked to the Source. It's a symbiotic relationship where our endeavors, bathed in divine favor, bear fruit that neither withers nor fades.

So, as you stand at the cusp of potential, teetering between the known and the vast expanse of the unknown, remember this: Your journey, while uniquely yours, is tethered to age-old principles. Harness them. They serve not just as a compass but as wings, propelling you into realms of success, influence, and impact that are beyond human comprehension.

Step forth with audacity, for you are not alone. With every stride, you carry the legacy of those who've gone before and the hope of generations yet unborn. The world isn't just waiting for what you create; it's yearning for the difference you will make. Embrace your call to dominion, and in doing so, pave the way for a legacy of greatness.

What are your growth goals?

How do you plan to multiply ?

CHAPTER 11 - IN THE IMAGE OF GOD

"And God said, Let us make man in our image, after our likeness: and let them have dominion over the fish of the sea, and over the fowl of the air, and over the cattle, and over all the earth, and over every creeping thing that creepeth upon the earth.So God created man in his own image, in the image of God created he him; male and female created he them." Genesis 1:26-27

Genesis 1:26 stands as one of the most profound declarations in the biblical narrative: **"And God said, "Let us make man in our image, after our likeness. Let them have dominion over the fish of the sea, the birds of the air, and over every living thing."'** This verse not only signifies the pinnacle of God's creative work but also establishes a foundational perspective for all human creators. Delving into its depths provides a tons of insights for artists, innovators, thinkers, and makers across time.

1. Imago Dei: The Divine Image in Humanity

The assertion that humans are made in the "image" and "likeness" of God (often termed the "Imago Dei") implies a reflection of the Creator's attributes in humanity. It doesn't suggest a physical resemblance but rather denotes attributes such as intellect, morality, and agency. In other words, just as God has the capacity to think, feel, and act purposefully, humans, too, possess these qualities.

For creators, this is a powerful revelation. It suggests that the innate drive to create, innovate, and express isn't just a biological or social construct; it's a divine endowment. The painter who brings landscapes to life, the writer weaving intricate narratives, the scientist unravelling nature's mysteries, or the entrepreneur shaping innovative solutions are all tapping into this divine image, manifesting aspects of the Creator's genius.

2. Dominion and Stewardship: The Creator's Responsibility

Genesis 1:26 doesn't merely emphasize humanity's royal status; it confers a responsibility. The term **"dominion"** might be better understood not as domination or exploitation, but as **stewardship**. It's about guiding, nurturing, and preserving. Creators, in a way, have dominion over their creations, bearing the responsibility to ensure that their works serve a greater good, benefiting society and the environment.

Artists, for instance, have the power to influence thought and culture. Entrepreneurs and technologists can reshape societal structures. This dominion mandates them to be conscious of the ethical implications of their creations. Just as God's act of creation was geared towards order, beauty, and harmony, human creators are called to ensure their works resonate with these divine principles.

3. Collaboration: The Collective Aspect of Creation

The plurals "us" and "our" in Genesis 1:26 have been a point of theological discussions. While interpretations vary, one perspective is that it alludes to a divine council or a heavenly assembly. Transposed to a human context, it suggests the importance of collaboration in the creative process.

No creation exists in isolation. Even the seemingly solo endeavors are built upon the foundations laid by predecessors or in dialogue with peers. The best of creations often arise from collaborative efforts, where diverse skills and perspectives merge to forge something unique and impactful.

4. Purpose-Driven Creation: Beyond Aesthetics

The creation narrative culminates with a world imbued with purpose. Every element, from the stars to the seas, plays a role in the grand cosmic design. For human creators, this underscores the need for purpose-driven creations. Beyond aesthetics or commercial value, creations should ideally serve a deeper purpose, addressing real-world issues or evoking meaningful emotions and reflections.

For a filmmaker, it could mean crafting stories that shed light on societal issues. For an architect, it could translate to designing sustainable and inclusive spaces. Every act of creation carries the potential to contribute to a larger narrative, echoing the grand design of the initial Creator.

Genesis 1:26 isn't just a theological proclamation; **it's a charter for all creators**. Recognizing the divine image within and the responsibilities it entails can elevate the creative process. Whether you're sketching a piece of art, penning a novel, designing a product, or innovating a new technology, remembering this divine mandate can guide you towards creations that don't just reflect human ingenuity but resonate with the divine harmony of the universe.

Divinity in Humanity: The Three O's

When it comes to understanding the image of God, God's attributes lay the foundation for comprehending the entirety of His essence. His **omnipresence**, **omniscience**, and **omnipotence** are mirrored, to some degree, in humanity. While we don't command the universe or know all things, within us burns a reflection of these divine attributes. Our continuous quest for knowledge, a fervent desire for power, and a profound need for connection all resonate with these divine traces.

However, beyond these godly attributes, humans also carry within them the seeds of divinity that are not as overtly powerful yet are deeply significant. The ability to appreciate beauty, for instance, seems to echo the Creator's penchant for magnificent sunrises or sprawling landscapes. Furthermore, our innate sense of morality, though not always aligned perfectly with divine standards, suggests an internal compass pointing towards a higher moral reality.

This reflection is also seen in our drive for achievement. Humanity's skyscrapers, technological marvels, and masterful artworks might be understood as an attempt to emulate the Creator's grandeur, showcasing our need to express, create, and leave a lasting imprint, just as God did with the universe.

God's Moral Footprint

Peering into the moral fiber of God offers further understanding of His character. His relationships and dialogues throughout biblical narratives, such as those in Exodus, provide deep insights into His essence: an interplay of justice and mercy, strength and compassion. Moses's divine encounter wasn't merely a meeting; it was a revelation of God's multidimensional nature.

In Exodus 33:18-19, Moses requests to see the glory of God.This was God's response in verse 19

> *"And he said, I will make all my goodness pass before thee, and I will proclaim the name of the Lord before thee; and will be gracious to whom I will be gracious, and will shew mercy on whom I will shew mercy."*

In Exodus 34:6-7 God passes by Moses, declares his name .

"And the LORD passed by before him, and proclaimed, The LORD, The LORD God, merciful and gracious, longsuffering, and abundant in goodness and truth,Keeping mercy for thousands, forgiving iniquity and transgression and sin, and that will by no means clear the guilty; visiting the iniquity of the fathers upon the children, and upon the children's children, unto the third and to the fourth generation."

Here God reveals His character to all of us, and we have a comprehensive sneak peek into His moral attributes.

From this narrative, we can see two main aspects when it comes to God's character. Primarily we see that He is merciful, but also, we see that He is just.

This insight is confirmed in the book psalms - Psalm 89:14 (KJV):

"Justice and judgment are the habitation of thy throne: mercy and truth shall go before thy face."

This scripture beautifully portrays the balance of God's nature. While His throne (representing His reign and rule) is founded on justice and judgment, He approaches us with mercy and truth.

The biblical narrative of creation captures a profound principle in its declaration:

"So God created man in his own image, in the image of God created he him; male and female created he them."

This simple yet profound statement has layers of depth that

beckon exploration. The very act of dividing humanity into male and female forms points to a deeper truth about the nature of God and His intentional design. The duality of male and female is not a mere biological distinction but a theological one, embodying and reflecting the dual nature of God Himself.

Drawing from the creation narrative, it's evident that neither the male nor the female alone can fully encapsulate the image of God. Their collective existence, their interdependence, and their complementarity are what provide a fuller representation of the Divine. It prompts the question: What is it about the union of male and female that other pairings cannot replicate? The foundational answer lies in the portrayal of God's dual attributes - His mercy and His justice.

Men, in their inherent nature, often exhibit qualities of firmness, strength, and assertiveness. These characteristics, while not exclusive to men, tend to be more pronounced in men and are a reflection of the justice side of God. This justice is not merely punitive but is deeply rooted in uprightness, order, and fairness.

On the other hand, women, in their essence, frequently exude tenderness, empathy, and nurturing care. These traits, reminiscent of God's grace and mercy, play a pivotal role in fostering connection, compassion, and healing. Again, while these qualities are not solely confined to women, they tend to be more prevalent in women, echoing God's merciful nature.

It's essential to recognize that these distinctions do not pigeonhole either gender into rigid categories. Men are just as capable of showcasing mercy, and women can wield justice with equal might. The point of this duality is not about creating stereotypes but about highlighting the complementary nature of these divine attributes as they manifest in humanity. Just as God's nature balances mercy with justice, the union of male and female balances strength with tenderness, order with nurture, and authority with compassion.

In physiological and emotional dimensions, this balance becomes evident. The physical differences between men and women are not just for procreation but also serve as a metaphor for their distinct roles in echoing God's image. Emotionally, the interplay of feelings and perceptions between genders often results in a harmonious balance, creating a holistic environment for growth, learning, and mutual edification.

In conclusion, the intentional design of male and female is not a mere biological afterthought but a profound theological statement. It serves as a reminder that, in our quest to understand and emulate the Divine, we must acknowledge, appreciate, and celebrate the duality and complementarity embedded in our very being. The dance of male and female, in their mutual respect and unity, paints a beautiful portrait of God's image - a blend of justice and mercy, strength and tenderness, authority and grace.

Delving deeper, this divine balance between justice and mercy serves as an essential guidepost for human interactions. When individuals or societies gravitate too far towards strict justice, they risk becoming cold and uncompassionate. Conversely, when there's an overemphasis on mercy, accountability might be lost. Thus, the divine balance offers a template for harmonious coexistence.

The duality inherent in God's nature permeates life at multiple levels. Take politics, for instance. Conservatism and progressivism, while often at odds, both possess elements echoing God's dual nature. The synergy of these forces, when recognized, has the potential to push societies towards unparalleled growth.

Further, this duality is apparent in economic systems. Capitalism, with its emphasis on individual achievement and reward, mirrors the justice aspect, while socialism, with its focus on community welfare and shared resources, reflects mercy. A balanced society might thus extract and integrate the best from both systems, aiming for both prosperity and equity.

The arts, too, reverberate with this balance. Music, literature, and visual arts often oscillate between evoking discipline and structure and invoking free expression and emotion, beautifully encapsulating the balance of the divine attributes of justice and mercy.

The Creator Within

Our creation in God's image is both a privilege and a responsibility. It signifies not only our inherent worth but also the potential for greatness. By blending imagination with the boundaries of reality, innovation with preservation, and individual expression with collective welfare, we mirror the Creator's balance in our endeavors.

Our ability to forge deep connections – be it in relationships, communities, or with nature – is a testament to our divine origin. These connections, when nurtured, don't just sustain us; they elevate our existence, allowing us to glimpse the interconnectedness of all creation, reflecting God's grand tapestry.

Our endeavors in science and technology, while seemingly secular, are often spiritual quests in disguise. By unraveling the mysteries of the universe, finding cures for ailments, or building tools to improve human life, we echo the Creator's initial act of bringing order from chaos, light from darkness.

Final Reflections

Genesis 1:26 is more than scripture; it's an introspective lens. As we navigate life's multifaceted journey, we must remember our divine heritage and seek to uphold it. Every skill, every interaction, every dream is an echo of this celestial legacy.

In moments of doubt or adversity, reflecting upon our divine origin can provide solace and direction. For embedded within us are the principles of balance, purpose, and creation that can guide us towards fulfilling our highest potential.

In celebrating our achievements, nurturing our relationships, and respecting our environment, we do more than just live; we magnify the divine image within, acting as beacons of light, reflecting the infinite brilliance of the Creator.

How will you reflect the image of God in your brand, business , product/ services?

CHAPTER 12 –THE
TOWER OF BABEL

"Wisdom is the principal thing; therefore get wisdom: and with all thy getting get understanding." Proverbs 4:7

S o far in this book, I've mainly restricted myself to Genesis 1 and 2 mostly, In these two chapters, I have outlined the concepts and blueprint of God's creative success. However, this is just the beginning. God's creative success and blueprint expand throughout all the scriptures, from the text of Genesis to Revelation. Within these pages, we observe God's blueprint, patterns, prophecies, prayers and promises, to mobilize us to what God calls us to be and do as creators and citizens of the kingdom.

In this chapter, we will delve deeper into principles that are not only found in Genesis chapter 1 but are interwoven throughout the entire Book of Genesis and continue to resonate throughout the Bible.

To begin with, our attention is directed toward Genesis 11, a passage that unfolds after the floodwaters had receded and mankind began to multiply and repopulate the Earth. We read:

"These are the generations of Noah: Noah was a just man

and perfect in his generations, and Noah walked with God."
- Genesis 6:9

From Noah, three dominant families emerged. These families dispersed, each charting its course and settling in various regions. However, one family's journey provides us with a compelling narrative that underscores a principle found repeatedly in the Bible.

"And the whole earth was of one language, and of one speech. And it came to pass, as they journeyed from the east, that they found a plain in the land of Shinar; and they dwelt there." - Genesis 11:1-2

The family, upon settling in Shinar, embarked on an ambitious project. Driven by their own aspirations and desires, they proclaimed:

"Come, let us build us a city and a tower, whose top may reach unto heaven; and let us make us a name, lest we be scattered abroad upon the face of the whole earth." - Genesis 11:4

Here, the motive is clear. This wasn't just about constructing a tower for shelter or community purposes, but it was to make a name for themselves, to establish their own legacy. It was an endeavour driven by pride and self-promotion.

This chapter in Genesis presents us with a paradigm of human endeavours. Throughout history, humans have often been driven by self-centred desires, seeking personal gain and motivated by their own ambitions. This perspective contrasts with many teachings in the Bible, which advocate humility, selflessness, and reliance on God's will:

> *"Pride goeth before destruction, and a haughty spirit before a fall." - Proverbs 16:18*

The Tower of Babel reminds us of the potential pitfalls of ego-driven aspirations and offers a lesson in the importance of aligning our purposes with that of God's.

As we continue, we will see how this principle of self-centeredness versus God-centeredness plays out in various narratives and teachings throughout the scriptures.

In contrast, we encounter Abraham's story in the subsequent chapter.

Genesis 12:1-3 (KJV) tells us:

> *"Now the Lord had said unto Abram, Get thee out of thy country, and from thy kindred, and from thy father's house, unto a land that I will shew thee: And I will make of thee a great nation, and I will bless thee, and make thy name great; and thou shalt be a blessing: And I will bless them that bless thee, and curse him that curseth thee: and in thee shall all families of the earth be blessed.*

This covenant that God makes with Abraham (then called Abram) isn't just a promise of personal blessing; it's a larger vision where Abraham would become a conduit for God's blessings to the entire world.

This juxtaposition between the Tower of Babel's story and Abraham's call from God illustrates a profound lesson on motivation. On one hand, there is the human urge for self-glorification, as seen in Babel. On the other, there is a divine invitation to be part of a grander plan, as seen in Abraham's life. Both may seem to lead to greatness or recognition, but the heart behind them is significantly different.

Abraham's journey is not about a self-initiated pursuit of personal prominence. Instead, he responds to God's call, becoming a vessel to spread blessings. It's a testament to the idea that true greatness stems from selflessness, serving a purpose larger than oneself, and aligning one's will with that of the divine.

This distinction is crucial in evaluating business models, creative enterprises, and strategies. If your venture only serves your personal interests, it lacks real value. Such ventures are unsustainable. In Abraham's case, his greatness stems from being a blessing to others, not self-serving pursuits. Success, therefore, lies in benefiting the greater community, thinking in terms of the families of the earth. This mindset is essential for both businesses and individuals – targeting an ecosystem or community rather than individual gain. This approach results in exponential growth, not just by a factor of 30 or 60, but even more.

While the story of the Tower of Babel already has a negative connotation, it offers myriad lessons, especially for creators.

1. Power of a Unified Language and Vision:

> - "And the whole earth was of one language, and of one speech." (Genesis 11:1, KJV)

The beginning of Genesis 11 highlights the power of a unified language. When everyone spoke the same language, they were able to communicate effortlessly, fostering understanding and collaboration.

2. The Significance of Communication:

- *"And they said one to another, Go to, let us make brick, and burn them thoroughly. And they had brick for stone, and slime had they for mortar." (Genesis 11:3, KJV)*

This verse highlights the ease with which people communicated their intentions and executed their plans. Effective communication is the bedrock upon which any successful venture is built.

3. **Uniform Vision**:

- *"And they said, Go to, let us build us a city and a tower, whose top may reach unto heaven; and let us make us a name, lest we be scattered abroad upon the face of the whole earth." (Genesis 11:4, KJV)*

The people had a collective goal: to build a tower reaching the heavens. This vision, backed by a unified language, was the driving force behind their project. The importance of having a cohesive vision is essential for creators as it provides direction and purpose.

4. **God's Perspective on Unity**:

- *"And the LORD came down to see the city and the tower, which the children of men builded. And the LORD said, Behold, the people is one, and they have all one language; and this they begin to do: and now nothing will be restrained from them, which they have imagined to do." (Genesis 11:5-6, KJV)*

The narrative showcases that there is potential danger in unchecked unity and ambition. God acknowledges the immense power of unity combined with a shared vision. The story underscores the idea that while unity and vision are powerful, they need guidance and checks to ensure they are used rightly.

5. **The Introduction of Diverse Languages**:

> *"Go to, let us go down, and there confound their language, that they may not understand one another's speech." (Genesis 11:7, KJV)*

God's intervention in confounding their language symbolizes the need for diversity and divergence in human societies. Yet, it also emphasizes the value and power of understanding – when people don't understand each other, their ambitions can be halted.

Genesis 11, despite its negative undertones, offers profound insights for creators. It underscores the power of communication, the importance of a shared vision, and the necessity for checks and balances in collective endeavours. Whether in ancient times or the present, the principles of communication and vision remain timeless.

In Genesis 12, we encounter a pivotal moment in Abraham's life and the unfolding story of God's relationship with mankind.

> *"Now the LORD had said unto Abram, Get thee out of thy country, and from thy kindred, and from thy father's house, unto a land that I will shew thee." (Genesis 12:1)*

Here, God's call to Abraham underscores the necessity of stepping out of one's comfort zone. Abraham, who was then known as Abram, was not merely asked to shift residences within familiar territory. Instead, he was called to leave everything he knew - his country, his family, and his father's house - for a land that was yet to be revealed to him.

The immediate promise that follows this divine directive illuminates the rewards of such faith-driven ventures:

"And I will make of thee a great nation, and I will bless thee, and make thy name great; and thou shalt be a blessing." (Genesis 12:2)

By venturing beyond the familiar, Abraham laid the foundation for a lineage and a nation that would forever change the course of history. It's a potent reminder that growth occurs when we dare to move beyond our comfort zones. Just as a seed must be buried in the ground to sprout and grow, you must be "planted" in new environments or situations to truly flourish.

James, in the New Testament, reminds us of the blessings that come with enduring tests and challenges:

"Blessed is the man that endureth temptation: for when he is tried, he shall receive the crown of life, which the Lord hath promised to them that love him." (James 1:12)

This principle of venturing into the unknown and facing challenges aligns with God's overarching plan for us. By trusting in God and daring to step outside of what is familiar and comfortable, we participate in the broader divine narrative that champions growth, faith, and expansion.

How can you make sure that your brand and business is not driven by selfishness but by selflessness?

CHAPTER 13 - THE GOLD OF THAT LAND IS GOOD

"And the gold of that land is good: there is bdellium and the onyx stone."-Genesis 2:12

Genesis 2 paints an evocative picture of Eden, the garden of delight. In this garden, God provided every single thing man would ever need, not just for survival but also for optimal existence. From the breath of life to the very ground he walked upon, everything was a testament to God's abundance. Yet, beyond these tangible blessings, one of the less spoken-about endowments bestowed upon man by God was the innate desire and ability to seek wealth and resources.

In Eden, the very concept of wealth was different. Here, God was the singular value, an omnipresent essence that filled every nook and cranny. Adam and Eve lived in such abundance that the very notion of lacking something was alien. The environment was laden with intrinsic value and divine energy. Everything had worth, not because of its rarity or its demand, but because God deemed it so.

However, the fall of man brought about a paradigm shift. It was not just the introduction of sin, but also the concept of lack. The devil's deception shifted Eve's focus from abundance to lack. This was the inception of the perception that they didn't have everything they needed.

With the advent of lack, the need for systems to measure and exchange value became evident. While in the beginning, there was an omnipresent value that God embodied, the fall brought about a need to have tangible representations of value. This birthed the barter system where goods were exchanged for goods, a primal and straightforward system of trade. Yet, as societies expanded and needs became more complex, bartering wasn't enough.

Precious metals then became the go-to medium of exchange. Gold, silver, bronze, and other metals began to be seen as standardized representations of value. These metals, especially gold, were not just instruments of trade but were also symbols of God's unchanging nature—rare, durable, and timeless.

The book of Daniel, specifically chapter 2, provides a profound allegory of world empires through Nebuchadnezzar's dream, which Daniel interprets. The statue in this dream, made of various metals, offers a layered understanding of not only the political might of these empires but also their economic characteristics.

1. **Babylon (Gold)**: "Thou art this head of gold" (Daniel 2:38). Historically, the Babylonian Empire, represented by the head of gold, is emblematic of the significance of gold in its economy. Gold was an essential medium of exchange in ancient Babylon. They used gold as money and for trade, showcasing their economic prosperity and stability. The opulence and grandeur of the Babylonian Empire are well documented, with gold being central to their wealth and economic system. Hence, the dream's representation of Babylon by gold is apt.

2. **Medo-Persian (Silver)**: Following the golden age of Babylon was the Medo-Persian Empire, represented by the chest and arms of silver in the dream. Historically, silver became a dominant currency during this era. The Persians introduced a standardized system of coinage, the most famous being the silver Siglos. This shift to silver from gold might hint at the changing economic dynamics, where silver played a more prominent role in trade and commerce, even though it's of lesser value than gold.

3. **Grecian (Bronze)**: The Grecian empire, symbolized by the statue's belly and thighs of bronze, offers another shift in economic currency. Alexander the Great, after his conquests, introduced a widespread system of coinage in the territories he ruled. Bronze, alongside silver, was heavily used for minting coins in the Grecian empire. The ubiquity of bronze coins, due to their lesser value compared to silver and gold, made them commonplace for everyday transactions.

4. **Roman (Iron)**: "And the fourth kingdom shall be strong as iron..." (Daniel 2:40). The Roman Empire, represented by the legs of iron, is synonymous with the might and reach of its rule. Economically, while the Romans used gold and silver for their high-denomination coins, they heavily relied on iron for their lower denomination coinage, especially during certain periods when economic challenges necessitated the minting of iron coins. These coins, although less valuable, were practical for everyday commerce, mirroring the expansive and intricate trade network of the Roman Empire.

Certainly, the feet of the statue in Nebuchadnezzar's dream, made of iron mixed with clay, hold significant meaning in the interpretation provided by Daniel. This part of the statue adds depth to the unfolding prophecy and reveals further intricacies of the empires that would come.

5. **Feet of Iron Mixed with Clay**: The feet and toes, partly of potter's clay and partly of iron, represent a divided kingdom.

Daniel 2:41-43 explains, "And whereas thou sawest the feet and toes, part of potters' clay, and part of iron, the kingdom shall be divided; but there shall be in it of the strength of the iron, forasmuch as thou sawest the iron mixed with miry clay. And as the toes of the feet were part of iron, and part of clay, so the kingdom shall be partly strong, and partly broken. And whereas thou sawest iron mixed with miry clay, they shall mingle themselves with the seed of men: but they shall not cleave one to another, even as iron is not mixed with clay."

This depiction of iron mixed with clay has been a subject of much discussion among scholars. The iron can be seen as a continuation of the Roman influence into the European nations and modern world, but the clay introduces a new element, suggesting fragility and division. Historically, this can be interpreted as the later stages of the Roman Empire, which saw internal and external pressures, leading to fragmentation and ultimately its fall. The mixture of iron with clay implies an unstable alliance, where elements of strength (iron) are present, but also vulnerability (clay). The inability for the two materials to fully integrate suggests an empire or empires with inherent weaknesses, despite displays of strength.

In an economic sense, the Roman Empire's later years were marked by instability, with devalued currency, inflation, and complex trade challenges. The iron could represent the remnants of Roman economic and military might, while the clay might symbolize the brittle nature of its financial systems, leading to economic vulnerabilities.

The metals represented in Nebuchadnezzar's dream not only symbolize the progression of empires but also offer a deep insight into the economic strategies, currency usage, and trade dynamics of each era.

In the contemporary age, we see a combination of iron and clay, indicative of a fragile economic structure that's a blend of solid and brittle elements. This is reflective of modern economies, where we have strong economic pillars but also weak speculative bubbles, like certain cryptocurrencies that don't have tangible assets backing them.

Grounded Value in a Transient World

In today's rapidly evolving world, creators find themselves at the heart of a whirlwind of trends, technologies, and ever-shifting values. From the newest social media challenges to the latest design aesthetics, the terrain of creation is constantly in flux. Amidst this chaos, it becomes essential for creators to discern the transient from the eternal, the frivolous from the foundational. Understanding the deeper dynamics of value becomes not just a matter of professional efficacy but also of personal integrity and legacy.

The world's systems of value have indeed undergone seismic shifts throughout history. From barter systems to gold coins, from paper money to digital currencies, each epoch has had its distinct mode of trade and value. These systems were invariably products of their time, tailored to the societal, technological, and economic contexts they emerged from. However, as different as they were, each system was an attempt, successful or otherwise, to quantify and represent value.

Amidst these varied systems, the Genesis model stands out as an illuminating beacon. It harks back to a time when value was unambiguous and grounded. In the Garden of Eden, value wasn't determined by market dynamics or human whim. Instead, it was divinely ordained. Every leaf, every creature, every gust of wind carried intrinsic value because it was part of God's grand design. This model provides creators with insights into what true, grounded value might look like. It serves as a timeless reminder that while the manifestations of value change, its essence remains constant.

Thus, for creators, the call is clear. You have been endowed with the ability to bring ideas to life, to shape the tangible from the intangible. With this ability comes a profound responsibility: to forge assets that have genuine, inherent value. These aren't just products or artworks that cater to the current zeitgeist. Instead, they are creations that, much like the elements of Eden, carry value in their very essence.

In a world characterised with the next big thing, it might be tempting to ride the wave of fleeting trends. After all, these trends often promise quick recognition and lucrative rewards. However, the true calling of a creator transcends these ephemeral allurements. The aim should not just be to gain momentary applause but to create lasting, impactful assets. Assets that generations to come would cherish, that would stand as testaments to the creator's vision and commitment.

In conclusion, as you navigate the intricate labyrinth of contemporary creation, may you draw inspiration from the Genesis model. By grounding your work in true value, you not only honor your craft but also contribute to a legacy that resonates through time. You can indeed be the architect of a new Eden, a world where value is celebrated in its purest, most authentic form.

The land is not merely a patch of earth; it's a canvas for divine creation, a foundation echoing God's handiwork. Just as it is written in Genesis 2:7,

> *"And the LORD God formed man of the dust of the ground, and breathed into his nostrils the breath of life; and man became a living soul,"*

the earth is not just our origin but also the very soil from which dreams and aspirations can sprout.

Remember the words of God to Adam in Genesis 3:19,

"In the sweat of thy face shalt thou eat bread, till thou return unto the ground; for out of it wast thou taken: for dust thou art, and unto dust shalt thou return."

This not only signifies our mortality but also emphasizes the intrinsic connection between humanity and the earth. It's the land that sustains us, provides for us, and, in many ways, defines us.

In a world that is increasingly focused on intangibles and virtual realities, the real economy, the truest value, is buried deep in the sanctity of the ground. It is reminiscent of the promises God made to Abraham in Genesis 13:15,

"For all the land which thou seest, to thee will I give it, and to thy seed forever."

This land, this earth, is a testament to God's promise, abundance, and creation.

Creators who discern this profound connection do not merely create; they co-create with God, painting on the most divine canvas available. They understand that investing in tangible assets like land transcends mere economic gain.

It becomes a spiritual decision, drawing them closer to the paradisiacal design God envisioned in the Garden of Eden, as described in Genesis 2:8,

"And the LORD God planted a garden eastward in Eden; and there he put the man whom he had formed."

In conclusion, when we value land, not just as an asset but as a sacred gift from God, we align our creative energies with the Divine, weaving our dreams into the vast tapestry that began in Eden.

What assets are you going to create?

CHAPTER 14 -
CREATIVE EDEN

"And the LORD God planted a garden eastward in Eden; and there he put the man whom he had formed."Genesis 2:8

I n the realm of inspiration, no place surpasses the garden of creativity. Envision the early days of mankind: God places Adam and Eve in a garden of delight, not in a palace, stadium, or stage. The question then arises: What is it about a garden that inspires the Creator of all to make it humanity's first dwelling?

In many ancient traditions, the garden symbolizes paradise, not just because of its aesthetic beauty but also due to its embodiment of harmony and balance. Gardens are spaces of both rest and labour, serenity and life—a living testament to the dynamic balance that all creators strive for.

The initial environment was homogenous; there were no harsh conditions and no need for shelter. Beyond this, a garden is an illustrative book of God and the essence of who He is to us, the creatures. God reveals Himself through nature. Observing it, we understand Him, ourselves, and the essence of creation. This understanding becomes the fertile ground from which creativity springs forth, nurturing ideas that grow into tangible expressions of art and innovation.

God first tasks Adam and Eve with tending the garden—a lesson in responsibility and work ethic. Creativity requires diligence. This doesn't mean an endless grind; true work is purposeful and value-driven. And where better to learn about work's true meaning than in the garden? The repetitive acts of sowing, watering, and weeding in a garden parallel the discipline needed in creative endeavors, reminding us that consistency and care are vital to seeing a project to fruition.

The Spiritual Implication of Photosynthesis: Insights from Isaiah 55 and Matthew 13

Isaiah 55 is a profound chapter that draws parallels between the Word of God and the inevitability of nature. The verse,

"For as the rain and the snow come down from heaven, and do not return there until they have watered the earth..."

(Isaiah 55:10), beautifully encapsulates the concept. Just as rain nurtures the earth, so too does God's Word water our souls, ensuring it brings forth life and does not return void.

The process of photosynthesis requires water and light to transform simple substances into life-sustaining nourishment. Similarly, when we absorb God's Word—His promises, commands, and assurances—we undergo a spiritual 'photosynthesis'. His words act as the essential components, and our faith, the catalyst. Together, they produce fruits of righteousness, wisdom, and compassion in our lives.

In Matthew 13, Jesus introduces the parable of the sower, illuminating the different outcomes of seeds based on where they fall. This parable can be intertwined with our understanding of photosynthesis. The seeds are God's words or teachings, and the types of ground represent the conditions of our hearts.

- The path where birds come and eat up the seeds is like a heart closed off to understanding, where the word cannot take root.
- The rocky ground, where seeds sprout quickly but wither away, mirrors those moments of fleeting enthusiasm without depth
- Among thorns, the seeds represent God's words choked by worldly concerns and desires.
- However, on good soil, the seeds flourish, yielding a significant harvest. This soil reflects a heart that receives, understands, and internalizes God's teachings, leading to abundant spiritual fruit.

When we connect this with photosynthesis, the idea is vivid. The Word of God, like sunlight, can only foster growth when it's absorbed by receptive ground (a willing heart) and given the necessary components for growth—faith, understanding, and an environment conducive for spiritual maturation.

For the creative spirit, this metaphor is potent. When creators let God's Word penetrate their hearts—much like sunlight through leaves—they harness the energy to transform, innovate, and illuminate. Their works become a reflection of divine wisdom, infused with purpose and authenticity.

In the intricate dance of nature, photosynthesis offers a rich allegory for spiritual growth and creative transformation. Isaiah 55 and Matthew 13 augment this concept, urging us to be like fertile soil, absorbing God's teachings and letting them nourish our souls. Just as plants convert light into life, we too can transform divine inspiration into creations that resonate with His essence.

From the garden, we glean these other vital lessons:

1. **Interdependence**: Plants give us oxygen and food, and in turn, they benefit from the carbon dioxide we exhale. This symbiotic relationship teaches creators about mutual dependence, collaboration, and coexistence. Understanding this

dynamic reminds creators that no creation is an island; every piece of art, every innovation, relies on past traditions, current trends, and future aspirations.

2. **Growth and Resilience**: Plants showcase the beauty of growth both above and below the ground. For creators, this signifies the importance of visible achievements (like a finished project) and personal development (like mastering a new skill). Behind every blooming flower is a network of roots absorbing nutrients and water—a symbol of the unseen efforts and challenges faced during the creative process.

3. **Seasonality**: Just as gardens have seasons of planting and harvest, creators too have periods of ideation, creation, and reflection. This cyclical nature emphasizes the importance of patience, timing, and understanding that everything has its moment. Artists and innovators must respect their "winter" seasons, understanding that dormancy and rest are as critical to the creative process as active creation.

4. **Adaptation**: Plants adapt to their surroundings, showing resilience in various conditions. Likewise, creators must be versatile, ready to evolve based on feedback, and understand when to pivot in their projects. The true measure of a creator isn't how they act during times of success, but how they reshape and reorient during challenges.

5. **Nurturing**: A garden thrives when tended to with care, much like how creative projects prosper with attention and nurturing. This instills a lesson about the continuous investment of time, effort, and love in what we create. As the garden requires the right balance of sunlight and shade, creativity thrives in environments that offer both critique and encouragement.

6. **Biodiversity**: A garden's strength lies in its diversity. Different plants serve different purposes and contribute uniquely to the ecosystem. This teaches creators the value of diverse skills, perspectives, and ideas. Just as monocultures in agriculture are

vulnerable to pests and diseases, a lack of diversity in creative perspectives can stifle innovation.

7. **Harvesting**: Gardens teach the value of reaping what you sow. Creators must understand that results are borne of hard work and patience. But it's also about recognizing when to harvest, realizing that waiting too long can sometimes mean missing an opportunity while rushing might lead to unripe outcomes.

8. **Roots and Foundation**: The strength of any tree lies in its roots. A creator's foundational skills, principles, and values define their growth trajectory and eventual success. These roots anchor us, ensuring that while we may sway with external influences, we remain true to our essence.

9. **Natural Rhythms**: Gardens adhere to nature's rhythm, emphasizing that there's a time for everything—a time to brainstorm, a time to execute, and a time to review. Respecting these rhythms allows creators to harness their energy efficiently, aligning their actions with their internal and external environments.

10. **Symbiosis with Nature**: The garden environment—soil, water, air, and sunlight—provides essential elements for growth. Similarly, creators need the right environment, resources, tools, and encouragement to flourish. By seeking environments conducive to growth, creators position themselves for optimal output and innovation.

11. **Transience and Permanence**: While flowers may wilt, the seeds ensure continuity. This underlines the importance of legacy in creation—what you create today can inspire generations tomorrow. Every creation leaves a mark, an imprint, reminding future creators of past visions and dreams.

Drawing from these lessons, as a creator you should immerse yourself in your projects as a gardener does in their garden, understanding that creativity is a journey, not just a destination.

A garden is a living entity, ever-evolving, much like the creative process. As seasons change and new plants grow, so does the gardener's understanding and connection to their space. Similarly, as creators, our relationship with our work transforms as we evolve, ensuring that every piece we create is a reflection of our ever-changing self.

In conclusion, the garden, in all its natural splendour, mirrors the intricate dance of creation. It's a testament to God's design, emphasizing mutual growth, patience, resilience, and the inherent beauty of the creative process. As you embark on your creative endeavours, may you always find inspiration in these timeless lessons from the garden of creativity. Remember, the garden isn't just about what it produces but the process of nurturing and growth. Embrace this journey with all its highs and lows, for therein lies the true essence of creativity.

What principle from the garden, stands out to you and why?

CHAPTER 15 - BUSINESS AS MINISTRY

"And the LORD God took the man, and put him into the garden of Eden to dress it and to keep it."Genesis 2:15"And I will bless them that bless thee, and curse him that curseth thee: and in thee shall all families of the earth be blessed."Genesis 12:3

In the vast realm of creation and commerce, the lines blur between ministry and business. As creators molded in the image of God, we have a unique mandate and responsibility to leave a lasting imprint on the world. Our creations, the value we introduce to the marketplace, aren't mere solutions to contemporary issues. They echo the divine essence within us.

Our role as vessels for God's presence on Earth isn't about His limitations but rather our empowerment. While God has bequeathed dominion over this planet to humanity, it's through us that He interacts with the world.

The marketplace, often seen as a simple venue for trade, is more profound. It is a battleground, a place where the spiritual confrontations between good and evil, righteousness and deceit, and truth and illusion take place. As creators, we're more than bystanders; we're participants, choosing a side with every creation.

Consider the multitude of products launched daily. Each either strengthens the forces of good or aids the ascent of evil. As creators, we bear the weight of ensuring our creations address humanity's needs and resonate with divine harmony.

Understanding this deepens our sense of purpose. It's not solely about the traditional concept of ministry or serving others. Business itself has divine origins. God designed it as a beautiful interplay of mutual reliance. In this dance of value exchange, we find the interconnectedness of humanity. One's strength compensates for another's weakness, benefiting both the individual and the broader community.

However, a common hurdle for many creatives is selling their creations. Inherent self-doubt, feelings of inadequacy, or apprehensions might hold them back. Embracing the image of God within mandates recognizing and valuing one's creations. Knowing one's worth is paramount.

Selling isn't merely a commercial endeavor but a spiritual obligation. As Proverbs 11:26, states

> 'He that withholdeth corn, the people shall curse him: but blessing shall be upon the head of him that selleth it.'

This scripture speaks to the value and even duty of bringing forth what we have to offer for benefit others. Denying the world our gifts deprives it of potential value. Just as the one who withholds grain is seen unfavorably, so too might we be judged if we withhold our unique gifts and talents that could benefit others. When God grants an idea, it's more than just a fleeting thought; it's a divine nudge towards a purpose.

By recognizing this, we understand that it is our duty to bring it to life in the marketplace. In selling our gifts, we not only benefit ourselves but also enrich the world. Our offerings, whether they are products, services, or even intangible ideas, can have a profound impact on the lives of others. Therefore, embracing the act of selling, as underscored by scripture, can be seen as an act of service, sharing the blessings God has bestowed upon us with the world."

Money, though frequently misconceived by many, is inherently spiritual in nature. The Bible doesn't shy away from discussing money or material wealth; in fact, it offers countless verses that pertain to the subject. As Rabbi Daniel Lapin points out, the concept of wealth can be viewed as God's acknowledgment for serving and aiding others. This notion echoes the teachings of the Bible, where service and love towards others is highly valued.

In the Book of Proverbs, it says,

> "Honour the LORD with thy substance, and with the firstfruits of all thine increase: So shall thy barns be filled with plenty, and thy presses shall burst out with new wine" (Proverbs 3:9-10).

This highlights the idea that by offering to God from our earnings or resources, we're not only recognizing Him as the source of all our blessings but also inviting abundance into our lives.

The Bible teaches about the beauty of giving and its spiritual implications. Acts 20:35 quotes Jesus as saying, "It is more blessed to give than to receive." The essence of this ethos is the act of giving, for through it, we not only bless others but find ourselves blessed in return.

The Parable of the Talents in the Gospel of Matthew provides deeper insight into this subject. In this parable, servants are given talents (a unit of money) by their master. The ones who invest and multiply their talents are commended, while the one who hides his is rebuked (Matthew 25:14-30). This suggests that God values the wise use of resources, including money, especially when it leads to growth and benefits others.

Therefore, when viewed through a biblical lens, money is not merely a materialistic entity but rather a tool. It's a means by which individuals can bless others, and in doing so, align themselves with God's principles of abundance, service, and stewardship. The more we give in service to others, in alignment with biblical teachings, the more we stand to gain – not just materially, but spiritually and emotionally as well.

To ensure credibility and authenticity in our ventures, it's essential to meld ministry and business seamlessly. Our creations are more than mere art; they are solutions, contributions to the ecosystem, reinforcing our role as givers. n essence, while "Ministry as Business" underlines the inherent value in our creations, "Business as Ministry" serves as a reminder of our loftier purpose. Both are interwoven, beckoning us to create with purpose, responsibility, and divine intention.---

One can't help but explore the symbiotic relationship between the tangible and intangible realms of business and ministry. Each feeds off the other, laying the foundation for a world where both monetary and spiritual gains align harmoniously.

While businesses are often celebrated for their tangible successes —profit margins, market shares, and product launches—there is a spiritual heartbeat that pulses beneath the surface. Every business decision, from sourcing materials ethically to ensuring fair wages, is a choice between elevating good or perpetuating harm. The spiritual ramifications of these decisions often echo longer than their immediate fiscal impacts.

Conversely, ministry, while rooted in spiritual endeavours, requires the structural integrity of business to flourish. Long-term missions, outreach programs, and even the simple act of spreading one's message require funding, planning, and strategic thinking. Without the acumen of business practices, even the most well-intentioned ministries might find themselves constrained, unable to reach those who need them the most.

As creators, it's imperative to merge these realms seamlessly. The pursuit of profit should never overshadow our higher calling. Every product designed, every service offered, and every transaction made should resound with a sense of purpose and responsibility. This is the core of our calling as creators created in God's image. It's not merely about thriving in the marketplace, but about infusing it with God's essence at every opportunity.

Building on the wisdom of past entrepreneurs and spiritual leaders, one realizes that true success, be it in business or ministry, lies in a relentless pursuit of serving others. By focusing on the well-being of the community and the world at large, we inadvertently set the stage for our own prosperity. This self-sustaining cycle, where giving leads to receiving, is a testament to the divine blueprint that underpins our existence.

Therefore, as creators, our journey isn't limited to crafting masterpieces but extends to navigating the intricate dance of ministry and business. To truly shine in this dual role, we must continually educate ourselves, not just in the skills of our craft but in the ethos that governs the interplay of commerce and spirituality.

In conclusion, "Ministry as Business; Business as Ministry" isn't just a philosophy but a roadmap. It calls for a holistic approach to creation, urging us to look beyond the immediate and to envision a world where our actions, both big and small, ripple out, bringing both material and spiritual prosperity to all. As creators, this is our true north, guiding us toward a legacy of lasting impact.

How is your business a ministry and how is your ministry a business?

CHAPTER 16 –
SHABBAT SHALOM

*"And on the seventh day God ended his work which he had made;
and he rested on the seventh day from all his work which he had
made.And God blessed the seventh day, and sanctified it: because
that in it he had rested from all his work which God created and
made." Genesis 2:2-3*

After six days of intense creation, we are told that God rested.In God's rest, we are introduced to the principle of Sabbath and rest.

The Sabbath principle, while seemingly straightforward, holds profound depths that transcend the simple act of rest. This foundational principle holds the key to understanding the rhythm and intentionality of life, creativity, and purpose.

Following the six days of creation, God chose to rest on the seventh day. It is noteworthy that this wasn't because of fatigue or exhaustion, as God is omnipotent. Instead, His rest was a deliberate act, signalling the completion of His creative work. The seventh day, therefore, stands as a symbolic testament to the perfection and wholeness of God's creation. It signifies that God looked upon His work and deemed it complete and good.

Furthermore, God's choice to rest on the seventh day provides humanity with a model of rest and reflection. By establishing a day of rest after the labor of creation, God teaches the significance of balance and rhythm in life. Just as there is a time for work and activity, there should also be a time for rest and rejuvenation, not just for the physical body but also for the soul.

The blessing and sanctification of the seventh day is yet another profound message. To sanctify something means to set it apart for a holy purpose. In sanctifying the seventh day, God was establishing a precedent for mankind to remember, observe, and cherish this day as a day of rest, reflection, and connection with the Divine.

Implications for Creators

The narrative of creation and rest in the bible offers profound lessons for all creators. Firstly, it teaches about intentionality. Just as God was deliberate in every aspect of creation, creators, too, must approach their work with purpose and clarity. Every act of creation, whether it's art, literature, science, or any other field, should be imbued with meaning and intention.

Secondly the act of God resting on the seventh day teaches creators the importance of balance. It's a reminder that while the act of creation is fulfilling and important, there is also a need for moments of rest and reflection. To immerse oneself completely in work without moments of respite can lead to burnout and a loss of perspective. True creativity flourishes when there is a balance between work and rest.

Lastly, the sanctification of the seventh day underscores the sacredness of creation. Every act of creating, in its essence, is a divine act, a mirror of the original act of creation by God. Creators, therefore, are not just making things; they are participating in a sacred tradition that stretches back to the dawn of time. This realization brings a sense of reverence and responsibility to the act of creation, urging creators to approach their work with respect, humility, and a deep sense of purpose.

As humans who are created in the image of God, the act of creating is embedded deep within our DNA. Every invention, every artwork, every business model – these are all expressions of this innate drive to create. However, continuous creation without pause can lead to burnout.

Think of the great artists of history, from Leonardo da Vinci to Wolfgang Amadeus Mozart. Their lives were not just endless churns of work. They had periods of introspection, relaxation, and appreciation of their creations. They knew the importance of stepping back, reflecting, and letting their minds wander. This act of mental and spiritual wandering is where connections are made, where dots are joined, and where real innovation happens.

The Role of Reflection

Reflection is an essential part of the creative process. By reflecting on what one has made, a creator can assess its impact, gather feedback, and then iterate. Continuous creation without reflection can lead to a lack of direction and purpose. The Sabbath principle encourages this pause and reflection.

Dr. Daniel Levitin, in his book "The Organized Mind," discusses the importance of letting our minds wander and how it can lead to creativity and problem-solving. The Sabbath, in many ways, offers a scheduled opportunity for such productive wandering.

In an increasingly fast-paced world, where the lines between work and rest are blurred by technology and societal expectations, embracing the Sabbath principle is more relevant than ever. It's not just about rest but about recognizing our human limitations, recharging our batteries, celebrating our achievements, and aligning ourselves with a purpose higher than mere productivity. The Sabbath principle is God's gift to humanity, a divine blueprint for sustainable creativity and a life of purpose.

The Profound Essence of the Sabbath

The emphasis on rest is no minor matter in the eyes of the

divine; God has ardently outlined it as the 4th commandment. Exodus 20:8-11 reads:

> "Remember the sabbath day to keep it holy. Six days shalt thou labour, and do all thy work: But the seventh day is the sabbath of the LORD thy God: in it, thou shalt not do any work, thou, nor thy son, nor thy daughter, thy manservant, nor thy maidservant, nor thy cattle, nor thy stranger that is within thy gates: For in six days the LORD made heaven and earth, the sea, and all that in them is, and rested the seventh day: wherefore the LORD blessed the sabbath day and hallowed it."

Diving deeper into the implications of this commandment, we find an unmistakable linkage between the concept of the Sabbath and the ecosystem of enterprise and industry.

At its core, the Sabbath's observance demands a prior period of diligent productivity. To truly observe the Sabbath, or 'Shabbat', one must first engage in six days of constructive labour. The necessity of labour is not a mere obligation; it's interwoven into the very essence of the commandment.

God didn't mold passive spectators; He crafted beings of action and creativity. Echoing His actions, He envisions us molding our worlds for six days and then taking a rejuvenating rest on the seventh. Pastor Khethelo Mazibuko aptly puts it that the Sabbath emerges as a conference of creators, displaying their masterpieces – their own 'universes' and 'planets' so to speak. So, each Sabbath poses a profound question: "What have you manifested in your world?" ," What have you created for the past six days?"

So, where does the economic dimension fit into this spiritual paradigm? A nuanced examination of the commandment offers a revelation. While on a superficial level, it might seem the commandment merely addresses the worker, the laborer, or the recently emancipated Israelite, the actual verbiage suggests an economic undertone.

The Sabbath is directed at those in positions of responsibility and ownership - those who oversee sons, daughters, servants, livestock, and even foreigners within their domain. This imagery encapsulates God's vision for His followers: to be proprietors, not mere occupants; to lead, not merely to follow; to grant, not merely to receive. This conviction resonates in Isaiah 58:13, 14. Those who sincerely reverence His Sabbath, God promises, will be elevated to preeminence, basking in prosperity and leadership.

> *"If thou turn away thy foot from the sabbath, from doing thy pleasure on my holy day; and call the sabbath a delight, the holy of the LORD, honourable; and shalt honour him, not doing thine own ways, nor finding thine own pleasure, nor speaking thine own words:"*

> *"Then shalt thou delight thyself in the LORD; and I will cause thee to ride upon the high places of the earth, and feed thee with the heritage of Jacob thy father: for the mouth of the LORD hath spoken it." Isaiah 58:13-14*

A lingering question persists: Why don't many modern-day believers, the inheritors of this promise, visibly bear its fruits? The crux of the matter lies in the collective amnesia concerning the Sabbath. The global community has inadvertently marginalized its significance, overlooking that God's governance and economic architecture pivot around this very command.

Extricating the 4th commandment would render the Decalogue devoid of its divine essence and context. Without it, the remaining commandments could be replicated or appropriated by any entity. But the 4th commandment stands resolute and unique. It proclaims God as the ultimate Creator, a declaration no other being can replicate. It establishes His unmatched supremacy, designating the rest as beneficiaries of His grand design, dependent on His grace and wisdom.

The first form of depature from the sabbath was in the shift in the day of observance of the sabbath from the seventh day (Saturday) to the first (Sunday). This was done by organized religion, namely - the Catholic Church. And as a result today most churches worship on Sunday. For a more in-depth exploration on this topic, I recommend visiting www.thesabbathtruth.com, a resource that offers extensive insights on the matter.

However, an equally pressing concern is the manner in which many believers, even those who adhere to the traditional day of Sabbath, approach it. The full essence of the Sabbath seems lost on many, who observe it as a mere ritual without appreciating its profound impact on life.

A tangible testament to the economic and cultural ramifications of the Sabbath can be observed in the global success of the Jewish community. Their Sabbath observance, spanning from Friday evening to Saturday evening, isn't just a routine; it's a rich blend of customs and practices offering myriad benefits. Here are a few.

1. **Resilience and Discipline**: The observance of the Sabbath, with its strictures and limitations, fosters a unique discipline. Abstaining from regular work and daily routines strengthens resilience and teaches the valuable skill of delayed gratification, attributes which invariably pave the way for success.

2. **Rest and Introspection**: Beyond physical rest, the Sabbath offers a periodic respite for the mind. This routine rejuvenation optimizes productivity and efficiency. Coupled with deep introspection and reflection, it cultivates a life of mindfulness and purposeful decisions.

3. **Community and Connectivity**: More than an individual practice, the Sabbath is a collective experience. It knits families

and communities, fortifying social ties, offering emotional sustenance, and even inadvertently creating avenues for networking.

4. **Education and Enlightenment**: Jewish culture reveres the act of learning. The Sabbath, in many households, becomes a haven for reading, debating religious scriptures, and intellectual engagement. This ingrains critical thinking and nurtures an enduring passion for knowledge, which often translates into academic and vocational achievements.

5. **Moral Compass**: The Sabbath, in its essence, is also a weekly reminder of religious tenets and ethical guidelines. This moral compass, refreshed weekly, guides individuals in both personal and professional spheres, ensuring success anchored in integrity.

These principles encapsulated in the Sabbath observance are not just ritualistic but revolutionary for anyone engaged in creation and innovation. The Sabbath isn't merely a day off; it's an institution of mental clarity, divine connection, and holistic sanctification. It's an antidote to the relentless cacophony of modern life.

A scripture from Psalms encapsulates the spirit of the Sabbath succinctly:

> *"Be still, and know that I am God: I will be exalted among the heathen, I will be exalted in the earth." - Psalms 46:10.*

This scriptural wisdom suggests that genuine connection with the divine requires stillness. To fathom God's purpose and presence, one must transcend the mundane and embrace serenity. True understanding and communion with God arises in that sanctified silence. In the hush of the world's clamor, in the tranquility of the Sabbath, the divine voice resonates with unmatched clarity.The sabbath allows for this deep communion to take place.

There is a powerful spoken word poem that I love that I would like to end with here. It's by Jefferson Bethke, another person who inspired me to discover my purpose. It's entitled The Greatest Artist of All Time. There is a short chorus at the end of the singing that really communicates what I am about to say; here it goes:

> *Pick up your pen, write a song, lift up your voice and sing along. Raise your bow, and play an anthem to the King. Bring all your paintings and your poems, cast them down before the throne. You are the maker's handiwork, a living Masterpiece.*

So bring your creations before God and recognize Him as the sole creator; when we have this right relationship with God, our creations will be cosmic and astronomical, not just in this world but even in the world to come.

The Creator's Final Note

In this vast cosmic tapestry where stars and galaxies find their place, where planets have their orbits, and where every organism, from the grandest to the most minuscule, plays a vital role, God remains the unmatched Maestro of Creation. When we, as creators, align ourselves with this ultimate Designer, our creations won't just be earthly masterpieces but will ascend in grandeur and reach celestial heights.

Thus, as I draw the curtains on this exploration of God's unique blueprint for success, I extend my deepest gratitude to you for accompanying me on this transformative journey.

It is my sincere hope that these insights have not only enlightened your mind but have also ignited the divine spark within you. The image of God is etched within each of us, and I trust you now see it clearer than ever.

Fear and doubt have no place in the heart of a creator who knows their worth, their lineage, their divine mandate. Step boldly into your calling, realizing that the same hands that molded the galaxies and the vast expanses of the universe also intricately designed you.

For those of you who've felt a resonance with these words and are eager to delve even deeper, to finetune and harness your creative potential further, I am here to guide you personally.

Let's engage in an intimate Creator Coaching session tailored to cater to your specific aspirations and challenges, spanning anywhere from one to two hours.

I am genuinely thrilled at the prospect of helping you harness your creativity with absolute clarity, unwavering confidence, and unmatched competence. To craft not just as any creator but to **Create Like God**.

Ready to embark on this new chapter? You can book me here - and yes, pun very much intended!

As you close this book, let it not be the end but the beginning of a magnificent creative story. Until we meet again, I leave you with a heartfelt "Shabbat Shalom". Stand tall, create fearlessly, and let the universe marvel at your masterpieces.

How are you going to prioritise sabbath in your business and ministry?

REFERENCES:

1. Edlund, M. (2010). **The Power of Rest: Why Sleep Alone Is Not Enough. A 30-Day Plan to Reset Your Body.** HarperOne.

2. Catmull, E. with Amy Wallace. (2014). **Creativity, Inc.: Overcoming the Unseen Forces That Stand in the Way of True Inspiration.** Random House

3. Levitin, D. J. (2014). **The Organized Mind: Thinking Straight in the Age of Information Overload.** Dutton.

4. Walker, M. (2017). **Why We Sleep: Unlocking the Power of Sleep and Dreams.** Scribner.

5. Lapin, D. (2010). Thou Shall Prosper: Ten Commandments for Making Money.* Wiley, 2nd edition.

Business Secrets from the Bible: Spiritual Success Strategies for Financial Abundance

6. The Holy Bible, **The Book of Genesis**. King James Version.

   - The Holy Bible: King James Version. (n.d.). Genesis.

7. Sebag, R. (n.d.). **The Natural Order of Money.**

8. John, J. (2023). **Sleep Tight: The # 1 Secret to Achieving your Dreams.**

NEXT STEPS

1. Join the NiyotheGreatest Premium Creators
2. Book A Comprehensive Creator Coaching Session
3. Get Free Copy of the Genesis Workbook

LET'S CONNECT ON SOCIAL MEDIA

@NiyotheGreatest

1. Facebook
2. Instagram
3. Youtube
4. Twitter (X)
5. TikTok
6. Facebook Page
7. Website

ent.com/pod-product-compliance
LLC
A
0526
004B/1749